AMERICA, OIL, & THE ISLAMIC MIND

AMERICA, OIL, & THE ISLAMIC MIND

The Real Crisis Is the Gulf Between Our Ways of Thinking

MICHAEL YOUSSEF

ZondervanPublishingHouse

Grand Rapids, Michigan

A Division of HarperCollinsPublishers

134769

CONTENTS

PREFACE

In writing this book, I have deliberately chosen not to be scholarly or technical because I wanted to spare readers the need to constantly refer to a dictionary or a lexicon. I have used the Westernized spellings of Arab names most commonly found in popular American periodicals.

When a person writes a book of this nature it is inevitable that some people will complain. Some will say I have painted an unrealistic and improbable picture. Others may accuse me of a prejudiced viewpoint.

Yet I speak from an experience most Westerners haven't had. I grew up in the Middle East where Islam and Islamic practices permeated all areas of life.

I have tried hard to distinguish between Islam as a religious system and Muslims as people. I love the people who embrace Islam—many of them were my classmates, neighbors, and businesspeople.

I am glad to be able to write freely in my adopted home, the United States. Like millions of Americans, I came to this country from the Middle East and found here freedom and refuge. Deep love for this country compels me to write about the connections between America, oil, and the Islamic mind.

While I risk being misunderstood on my sociological, economical, or political assessments, it is my ardent desire that no one misunderstand my genuine love and deep appreciation for Muslim people.

From my perspective as a Christian, I see all other religious systems as less than whole. The God who revealed himself in the person of Jesus Christ tells us that without the one Savior, no one can be accepted to the Father.

I do not look down on Muslims. On the contrary, I yearn for them to know the fullness of life that comes only through Jesus Christ.

INTRODUCTION

On November 4, 1979, militant Iranian students invaded the United States embassy and other offices in Tehran and took fifty-two employees hostage. This act proved to be a dramatic turning point in America's understanding of modern Islam. "This is not a struggle between the United States and Iran," the Ayatollah Khomeini declared. "It is a struggle between Islam and the infidels." In other words, the Western way of life is anti-Islamic and should be viewed as an adversary of the Islamic way of life.

For more than a year there had been a barrage of headlines about the turmoil in Iran—the riots against the shah's regime, Khomeini's return from exile to lead a spiritual revolution, the horror of seemingly endless executions. Then came the hostage crisis. This was something different, and it struck a raw nerve in the American psyche. In the following days the suspicion deepened that Islam and its zealots were a threat not only to the lives of the hostages, but also to the peace of the world.

"The governments of the world should know that Islam cannot be defeated," Khomeini declared in August after he had thrown out the shah, executed many of his enemies, and inundated Iran with his style of revolution. "Islam will be victorious in all the countries of the world, and Islam and all the teachings of the Koran will prevail all over the world."

Non-Islamic countries listened with dismay. Cries of "Who is this Khomeini anyway?" gave way to "He's a madman" and "It makes no sense." Of course it didn't—not to the uninformed. But to Muslims it made perfect sense.

Khomeini's call for worldwide Islamic revolution gathered a million ayes, even though Islamic moderates wished he had not been so fanatically blunt. Some Arabs strongly support the establishment of a Palestinian state somewhere on the West Bank but at the same time are embarrassed by the various terrorist attacks of the Palestine Liberation Organization (PLO).

The true moderates are becoming a minority on the world scene. It is the extremist Muslims who grab the headlines. As never before, they are affirming their spiritual identity and flexing their political and economic muscles to promote the Islamic way of life. The spread of Islam today is greater than at any other point in history. Petrodollars and Islamic doctrine form an unprecedented power base on which to increase Islam's scope and influence. Islam is no longer "over there" in the Eastern hemisphere. Now it is on our doorstep.

In 1990, the Gulf Crisis not only brought Islam once more to our doorstep, it came through the door and all the way into the living rooms and bedrooms of most American families.

We have watched the tearful goodbyes as American fathers and mothers had to leave home in obedience to President Bush's call to go and defend the oil-rich fields of Saudi Arabia and to free Kuwait.

Saddam Hussein, who a short time ago fought a bitter eight-year battle against a mogul of the Iranian revolution, today robes himself with the Islamic mantle. He calls faithful Muslims everywhere for a *jihad*, a holy war.

Saddam Hussein sees the sheiks of Kuwait and Saudi Arabia as corrupt and says they are not "the true Muslims." He is not alone in his assessment. In his corner are millions of politically oppressed and economically harassed masses throughout the Arab world, many of whom have lived on the falling crumbs of these oil-rich sheiks.

Jihad, Islam, and Koran are relatively new vocabulary words for the average American, yet they are bound to be part of our daily dose of news for some time to come.

Because of propaganda blared at us, we in the West came to believe that Khomeini and his revolutionaries were villains. Now we call Saddam Hussein the villain. Who will be next? The simplistic assessment of news presented by Western media concerning the complex issues in Islamic countries is bound to confuse us.

Despite wide coverage, one aspect of the story has been ignored by reporters: In the past, Saddam Hussein has permitted freedom of religion while Saudi Arabia, beloved of the West, has forbidden Christians or Jews from having a place of worship anywhere on Saudi soil—even for foreign Christians and Jews! And the Saudi Arabian government does not permit anyone who is not Muslim to be a citizen. Those who visit Saudi Arabia

Iran vs. Saudi

must do so with strict conformity to these religious restrictions.

Perhaps you recall that Bob Hope went to Saudi Arabia to entertain American troops at Christmas. The government refused a visa to Brooke Shields, even though she promised not to flaunt American customs. She could not even get into the country to entertain soldiers there to protect Saudi interests.

This raises the common, persistent question: "Why are Muslims so fanatical about their religion?" Along with this I often hear another question asked, "Why is it that the more devout one becomes to Islam, the more intolerant that person becomes to other religions?"

From the viewpoint of Islam, Muslims believe they alone have been given "the final" revelation of God in the Koran. I say final because most Muslims respect the *Torah* (the five books of Moses) and the *Injeil* (their version of the Gospel). From the commands of their sacred book they are called to be the enforcers of God's will. For all its followers, whether moderate or zealot, young or old, religious or secular, Islam carries what some consider the harsh, intolerant imperative to convert or conquer unbelievers. To the Muslim idealist, there is no room for moderation. The recent political and economic wealth of so many Muslim countries is allowing this uncompromising side of Islam to manifest itself on a greater scale throughout the world.

Some observers fear that Western society increasingly is being faced with the challenge of real Islam. Dollars, weapons, oil, and any other commodities will be used to squeeze the enemy into surrender. For Muslim purists, non-Muslims are pawns in the holy war—the objective being to bring the world under the umbrella of Islamic control and thus, finally, to "fulfill God's will for all people."

If we want to understand critical, world-embracing events such as the Arab oil embargo, the Iranian revolution, and the Gulf crisis, if we want to develop a more intelligent foreign policy for the Middle East, if we want to better understand the impact of petrodollars on our own economy, we need to come to grips with Islam.

We must come to see that the political and economic actions of Khomeini or Saddam Hussein, the decisions of the royal family in Saudi Arabia, and the aggressive statements of Libyan strongman Moammar Khadafy and other Islamic leaders before him (such as Nasser) are rooted in Islam. The Lebanese war can be explained and understood only in terms of Muslims who are unwilling to tolerate Christian leadership of an Arab country. Muslims must dominate—hence, the civil war.

Most Westerners, steeped in the traditions of a separate church and state, have genuine difficulty comprehending this idea. Conversely, Muslims cannot differentiate between the Western way of life and the Judeo-Christian ethical systems. Even though the Judeo-Christian heritage has greatly influenced our standards and values, it is not exclusively identified as the whole. But to Muslims, America is synonymous with Christianity.

Historically, encounters between Islam and Christianity, both in their theological and political realms, have never been happy. The result has often been war. Muslims, who confess that there is only one true God and that Muhammad is his only true prophet, view Christians as blasphemers for proclaiming that Jesus Christ is the Son of God. Christians who have some knowledge of Islam often regard the religion of Muhammad as the religion of the sword. From a religious perspective, Christianity and Islam agree on one fundamental principle: God is Creator of all things. But beyond that point they agree on little else.

Islamic fundamentalism is not a new trend; it is not something that has blossomed in the last ten years. Landrum R. Bolling makes this clear:

> Islam, like other great religions, has had recurring periods of revivalism, interrupted by periods of quietism, decline and decay. The Muslim religion is now, evidently, entering another period of revival and renewal—and of assorted challenges to its non-Islamic neighbors. . . . This is a many faceted movement, with many different leaders and varying objectives. Khomeini did not start it and his passing will not stop it.[1]

These words, spoken more than ten years ago, have proven to be prophetic. Few people predicted that Khomeini's former enemy, Saddam Hussein, would be Khomeini's mantle bearer.

---

1 Landrum R. Bolling, "Islamic Fundamentalism on the Move," *The Saturday Evening Post* (September 1980), 54.

OPEC power may rise or fall. The price of oil may go up or down, yet Islam and fundamental Islamic ideology remain constant.

I want to emphasize that the principles discussed in this book are permanent. A temporary gain or loss in income will not slow the majority of the Islamic world in its drive to carry out its mission of chipping away at Christianity, which Muslims perceive to be their number one rival because of Christian missionaries, not only in the West, but also in Africa and parts of Asia. We must not think that the Islamic vision for a holy war will be affected by external circumstances such as the price of oil, although the black gold will do a lot to help them accomplish that mission.

I have written this book for those who want to know more about Islam. Let me repeat that what I seek to clarify is fundamentalist Islam and its modern approach to its original vision of spreading like a blanket over the globe. I do not hate any individual Muslim; many of them are my friends. Indeed, as our Lord commanded, I strive to love every person with the love of Christ.

CHAPTER 1

ON WESTERN DOORSTEPS

The largest portion of surplus oil money has been invested in the West—mostly in the United States.

*T*he instability the Middle East has experienced for the past few years has pushed it into the limelight of Western media. As a result, people in the West have become aware of some aspects of the Middle East, but they have not yet begun to understand the heart of the Middle East Islam.

Regional instability has little effect on the final mission of Islam, which is to invade the minds and hearts of every human being. Should the radical Muslim movement abate, the mission would not be diminished, for many of the so-called moderate nations of Islam are the ones who condemn Western materialism and spend billions of dollars in efforts to convert the West and bring it under their religious umbrella. Should the radical movement succeed in gaining control in any of the major oil-producing nations, the danger to the West will become more obvious and more immediate than it already is.

In a world economy dependent on oil, countries fortunate enough to possess a superabundance of the coveted black gold can become fantastically wealthy almost overnight. This is precisely what happened with the Arab oil-producing nations. If oil dependency had a negative effect on the world in general, quite the opposite was felt by nations belonging to the Organization of Petroleum Exporting Countries (OPEC). Their staggering profits skyrocketed from $50 billion in 1974 to $200 billion in 1980, and now it is over $1 trillion. In 1981, Saudi Arabia alone earned $110 billion from the sale of oil. In 1990, with the price of a barrel reaching nearly $40, thoughts of the net profit stagger the imagination.

What are the Arabs doing with all that money? Sensational headlines in the world press seem to indicate that the nouveau riche oil barons have nothing better to do with it than indulge their whims. Stories abound about Saudi Arabian princes casually gambling away millions of dollars in a single evening at European casinos, or more specifically, about the Arab sheik who tried to buy the Alamo as a birthday present for his son. These tales are outrageous and amusing, but are exceptions to the actual way the bulk of Arab oil profits are used.

The sparsely populated Arab member states in OPEC invested enormous amounts of money in domestic development programs, but they soon ran out of such uses for the vast sums pouring into their treasuries. The states reacted accordingly, and the money coming in was channeled into foreign investments, primarily in oil-consuming nations. As an example, Saudi Arabia is now estimated to have more than $150 billion invested in other countries. (Accurate figures are hard to come by due to the Saudis' desire to keep such information private.)

The largest portion of surplus oil money has been invested in the West—mostly in the United States. Publicity surrounding various Arab purchases of foreign land and business is often misleading since it generally focuses on localized issues and, therefore, does not reveal the full extent of Arab investment.

It is impossible to determine accurately the scope of Arab foreign investment because most of it is carefully concealed behind a screen of secrecy established through third party negotiations. And since the United States government does not know how much Arab money is involved in its economy, it has not yet developed an adequate system to either identify or control those investments.

The Kuwaitis, with their 4.9 percent ownership of some of America's top firms (assuming past Kuwaiti rates of investment),[1] have holdings just below the level at which disclosure to the United States Securities and Exchange Commission is required. American administrations for the past fifteen years have been nervous enough about Arab investments to refuse publication of incisive analyses of Arab holdings in the United States. The White House often claimed that disclosure would

---

1 See "Arab Banks Grow," *Business Week*, October 6, 1980, 70–84.

scare off other Arab investors. No wonder Saddam Hussein eyed his small neighbor for some time as the crown jewel of the neighborhood.

This Arabic economic offensive is even more alarming than the crisis originating with the oil embargo of 1973. If the oil embargo was seen as something the U.S. could cope with directly, the rise in Arab investments is seen by some as being a more hidden and controlling danger.

Arab investments are diversified in the United States. The Saudi Arabian Monetary Fund has quietly loaned billions of dollars to such U.S. corporations as American Telephone and Telegraph, International Business Machines, Dow Chemical, and Kimberly-Clark.[2] But Arab investors have also put money in American real estate, apartments, hotels, shopping centers, tourist resorts, and lands, banks, and other financial institutions.

Arab investors constantly seek new investment opportunities in America. Through Kuwait, for example, the Arabs attempted to set up loans for Lockheed, the once financially troubled United States aerospace giant. That company turned away from the Arabs when an agreement could not be reached assuring the company that the Middle Easterners would not control the corporation. The Arabs also pursued American Motors when it was preparing to ask the United States government for loan guarantees totaling $109 million. Accord-

_____

2 "Arab Banks Grow," 71.

ing to some financial insiders, this sort of maneuvering goes on all the time, although only one out of one hundred such attempts ever receives public attention. Nevertheless, a lot of investment hunting is under way.

Some influential Americans help with this investment hunting. Frederick G. Dutton, an assistant secretary of state in the Kennedy administration, has been a consultant for the Saudi Arabian government. Clark Clifford, a former secretary of defense and presidential advisor, became a partner in a law firm that is employed by the Algerian government. J. William Fulbright, at one time the chairman of the Senate Foreign Relations Committee, became associated with a law firm listed as an agent for the United Arab Emirates and Saudi Arabia.

It is no surprise that former United States government figures are consultants for Arab governments. Much of the OPEC investment in America is in the United States government itself. From 1974 to 1977, OPEC put 34 percent of its total American investment in United States Treasury securities; that amounted to $14 billion. Today this figure is estimated to be much higher.

Such high investment levels inevitably lead to the question of potential Arab pressure on the United States to alter policy on critical issues. We have now seen that when the Saudis felt Iraq could function as a buffer against the radical Iranian revolutionaries, they used their influence to push the U.S. to support Iraq in the Iran-Iraq war. Now the tables are turned. American men and women are risking their lives to defend the Saudis against their former ally and Arab brother, Iraq. At what point could Arab governments make threats of financial and oil disruption that, if carried out, would severely damage the economies of the United States and other Western nations? What pressure might be brought to bear on companies doing business with, or largely owned by, Arab governments that might influence decisions favorable to the Arabs?

Take the case of the Flour Corporation in Irvine, California. The company was involved in a $55 billion natural gas conservation project in Saudi Arabia when J. Robert Flour, the company's chairman, asked his stockholders and employees to support a Middle East arms package the Arabs wanted—a package proposed by the Carter administration.

The Muslim Ummah

Ummah is the Islamic concept of the "community of believers." Some Islamic experts see it as the foundation on which a Muslim common market could be established. If Europe can have its common market, why not the Arab states? Again, the danger lies in the nature of Islamic fundamentalism. Europe's common market exists for trade, not as a religious and political tool to convert or subjugate those not in accord.

The first Middle Eastern leader who flirted with this ideology and thus become the hero both of Moammar Khadafy and Iraq's Saddam Hussein was Gamal Abdel Nasser of Egypt.

Like Saddam Hussein, Nasser's ideology received a warm embrace from the masses of the Arab world. He did not get the same response from rich Arabs who saw themselves heading for the poor house under such Islamic socialism.

Alternatively, the oil-rich Muslim nations are uniting for the sake of the Ummah, but in order to preserve their wealth. While the radicals want the kind of common market in which all wealth is shared, the rich want a common market that insures the protection of their personal wealth. At the heart of the investment strategy of the wealthy Muslim countries is the vast international banking system the Arab OPEC nations are building. The practically unlimited financial resource of some of the Arab nations, coupled with all Western nations' increasing dependency on Arab money and Arab oil, give the Arabs a potential stranglehold over the West's economic destiny.

To a number of observers, the Arabs could threaten to capture control of the world's financial resources in the nineties the same way they took control of the world's energy resources in the seventies. The danger they feel is that development of the Arab banking system could mean a politicizing of international banking in a way that works against the interests of the West.

Such politicizing takes place because of the close relationships between the components of the Arab banking system and the Arab states themselves. United States corporations, such as American Telephone and Telegraph, International Business Machines, Dow

Chemical, Kimberly-Clark, and many others reportedly have received hundreds of millions of dollars in loans from the Saudi Arabian Monetary Agency. In those cases, that agency functions both as a bank and a facet of the Saudi Arabian treasury.

Kuwait also has its investments bank—the Kuwait Investment Office. In the early eighties it tried to buy 15 percent of Getty Oil for $15 billion. In doing so, it acted as an arm of the nation of Kuwait itself, just as it did when it bought 4.9 percent (as much as allowed without having to publicly announce its ownership) of virtually all the top twenty U.S. banks, plus sizable slices of Eastern Air Lines, Mobil, and Exxon.

Many heads of Western countries would be cautious if, in disclosing facts regarding Islamic investments in their countries, they would enable the populace to understand the significance of the financial bondage associated with such business dealings. Arabs are demanding, and getting, a voice in running some Western businesses. One European banker observes, "It took the Arabs ten years to learn how to wield their oil power, but it isn't going to take that long to wield their money power."[3]

Islamic centers are springing up all over the West. Mirza Khizar Bakht, Secretary-General of the First Interest-Free Finance Consortium, Great Britain's very own Islamic bank, dreams of establishing a Muslim shopping

---

3 J. B. Kelly, "Islam Through the Looking Glass," *The Heritage Lectures* (Washington: The Heritage Foundation, 1980), 8.

center in central London's Regent Street or in Knights-bridge. The aim of the center is to "unite the whole Muslim world in London."

Mirza Khizar Bakht's notion of London as a center of Islam is becoming a reality. The Islamic Council of Europe, based in London, spends large sums on propaganda among Muslims and Christians and has built mosques in each major European city. Already the Central Mosque in London raises its minaret into the English sky. Built at an estimated cost of $7.5 million, it seats 2,800 people. But this is only one of hundreds of mosques throughout England.

While London is a base of operations for expansion, the greatest number of European Muslims lives on the Continent. France has a Muslim population of over 3 million, West Germany follows with more than 2 million, and the number there is expanding as Islamic centers and schools are established. In Spain, leftists and environmentalists find it fashionable to be Muslim. In Rome, a new mosque was constructed at an estimated cost of $20 million.

While free to build Islamic centers of worship all over Europe, the Saudi government refuses to permit a single room to be used by Christians for Christian worship within Saudi Arabia.

The Ummah and the United States

The erection of Islamic mosques and the propagation of Islamic teachings are being pursued vigorously in the United States. In the eighties, Muslims purchased one thousand acres near Abiquiu, New Mexico, to build a model city of Islam. When finished, the town will house one hundred families and will include a seven-domed adobe mosque, a school, and a literature center. Saudi Arabia and other Muslim countries are spending tens of millions of dollars in community development and other projects throughout the United States. Their aim is to help the Muslim communities expand.

It is estimated that in the seventies Islam grew by 400 percent in the United States. Many Americans, predominantly blacks, are turning to Islam. They are rejecting values and ideals they consider outgrowths of a hypocritical white Christian society. When one black Muslim was asked why he had turned to Islam, he answered, "Christianity is a racist religion; Islam is a religion of peace." As contrary to historical fact as this statement may be, the thought has become dominant in the minds of many black Americans. Listening to Louis Farrakhan for a minute discloses the reality of what I am talking about.

The black Muslims in the United States have begun to integrate into the wider community of Orthodox Islam. The American movement has taken the title of "World Community of Islam in the West." Historically, black Muslim Americans have not been recognized by Orthodox Islam because of their belief in black supremacy and "other heresies." But under their present leadership, black Muslims are working to come to a meeting of the minds with the leadership of Orthodox

Islam. The number of Muslims in America is estimated at more than four million, a figure that is increasing rapidly.

Muslim membership in America comes from two sources—converts and immigrants. American converts to Islam seem to fall largely within the twenty- to thirty-year-old age group. They are mainly black American from lower income brackets. But an American church official estimates that 70,000 Caucasians turned to Islam between 1973 and 1983.

Since the late sixties, several important Islamic organizations have sprung up to strengthen and support American Muslims and to propagate their message and the practice of their faith. The Council of Imams trains local mosque prayer leaders, and the Association of Muslim Students has at least two hundred active chapters on college campuses in the United States. Those groups have equivalents in England, Australia, Canada, and other Western countries.

A brochure from the headquarters of the Association of Muslim Students in Plainfield, Indiana, describes the group's five top priorities as follows: (1) disseminating Islam through publications geared to both Muslims and non-Muslims; (2) establishing Islamic institutions, including places of worship, community service centers, and educational facilities; (3) assisting Muslims in practical aspects of religious observance (the five pillars of Islam); (4) propagating and facilitating Islam's faith-sharing effort among non-Muslims; and (5) encouraging the "unity of Muslim conscience" through a heightened sense of belonging and Muslim identity. With vast sums of money at their disposal, there is no doubt that Islamic Americans will be able to spread their message far and wide in the United States.

Few people realize how aggressive Islamic missions in the West are. Great Britain seems to be a special target for Islam. One Muslim leader declares that the United Kingdom is "ripe for conversion." There are at least three hundred mosques in Great Britain; some are former Christian churches. Also, Great Britain has twenty-two English-language newspapers that propagate Islamic teaching by various methods.

In 1976, the world's first Festival of Islam was held in England. It was opened by the Queen and lasted three months. The festival statement declared, "Unless we win London over to Islam, we will fail to win the whole of the Western world." As part of the festival, a missionary training center was opened, and Islam's intentions were made clear in a London press conference headlined, "Muslims Launch Missionary Crusade for Britain and the Rest of the World."

What Does It All Mean?

This chapter has provided an overview of two relatively recent and potentially very dangerous phenomena: (1) the investment of billions of Arab dollars in the American economy, and (2) the pouring of huge sums of money into aggressive Islamic evangelistic efforts in the West. The danger in the first case is that as Arab investment grows, Western economy will be increasingly dependent not only on their oil but also their money and will become vulnerable to disruption in the event of a fundamentalist revival.

The danger in the second case is perhaps more subtle, but its consequences could be even more devastating. We in the United States enjoy religious freedom. People of all faiths, including Islam, are at liberty to practice their religion and evangelize. As the followers of Islam increase their efforts to win the hearts and minds of the world, we must redouble our own efforts to reach the world with the gospel of Jesus Christ. By the same token, most Arab Islamic nations consider Christian missionary activity to be a crime and those involved in it are punished as criminals.

Numerous Muslims who converted to Christianity languish in prisons in North Africa and in the Middle East. Their crime? It was not converting to Christianity; it was forsaking Islam. But the penalty is sometimes more stiff. Forsaking what Muslims consider the only true religion is an offense punishable not only by imprisonment, but sometimes by death.

CHAPTER 2

OPEC AND ISLAM

The West, which makes a keen separation between business and religion, is generally ignorant of the close links between OPEC's controlling leadership and Islam.

*I*n the late twentieth century, the religion of Muhammad has blended with a new and powerful uprising of Arab nationalism. As a result, Islam has become not only a symbol of Arab culture, but also a potent expression of anti-Western sentiment. Couple this with the disturbing fact that oil-consuming nations are becoming subservient to wealthy, oil-producing nations, and the economic forecast for the West is not optimistic.

Nations who benefit from Arab money and aid must begin to take seriously Islamic religious influence and its imposition of conditions for the use of that money. Islam teaches that no Muslim should be answerable to a non-Muslim.

What would happen, then, to a company whose controlling interest was suddenly owned by Muslims? Would top management be replaced with Muslim personnel who would be accountable only to one another? Or suppose an American company were to demand that personnel convert to Islam to win a Middle Eastern contract. Too far-fetched, you say? Is it? There are signals that Western institutions are already giving in to Islamic demands to capture Arab petrodollars.

The West, which makes a keen separation between business and religion, is generally ignorant of the close links between OPEC's controlling leadership and Islam. A small but growing number of Westerners, however, are learning how Islam affects business practice.

Wade Kern, an airplane pilot and a Southern Baptist, sued Dynaelectron Corporation of McLean, Virginia, for firing him—allegedly because he would not convert to Islam. Dynaelectron, an engineering company, had won a contract to work at the Sacred Mosque in Mecca, Saudi Arabia. Thirty employees, on orders from the Saudi government, became Muslims so they could man firefighting helicopters during pilgrimages to the mosque. Kern refused to bend to the Saudi insistence that he become a Muslim. This refusal, he contends, is the reason he lost his job.

The nearly 400,000 American soldiers of Operation Desert Shield were told very plainly that if they wanted to celebrate religious holidays, they were to do so in remote areas where they would not be observed by the local citizens. Chaplains, both Christian and Jewish, were told not to wear their yamacha or crosses in public. This is the land of pure Islam. Any icon of another religion is an abomination. The practice of an infidel is an offense to Muslims. The Islamic stance also explains why neither a single Christian church or Jewish synagogue can be found in the whole country of Saudi Arabia.

Think of the irony. American soldiers are there to defend them and their enormous wealth, yet Islamic intolerance to Christians and Jews remains as severe as in the days of Muhammad 1400 years ago.

Moreover, Islamic nations have little reluctance about entering alliances with any of their brethren simply on the strength of the Muslim bond, no matter how questionable, even sinister, those alliances might be. Idi Amin, former ruler of Uganda, slaughtered an estimated 300,000 Christians and, when overthrown, slipped out of Uganda into the protective arms of his Muslim brothers in Libya and Saudi Arabia.

As the Arabs continue their massive investments in the West, they desperately want to avoid disclosure of their huge holdings in United States Treasury bills and bonds. Why? First, the more wealthy countries, such as Saudi Arabia and Kuwait, recoil at the fanaticism of the poorer hardline Muslim states such as Libya, Syria, Iran, Iraq, and above all the Palestinians. Generally, they feel that the less the radicals know about their business dealings, the better. Second, the Arab investors do not want the West to panic over an apparent Muslim economic invasion and thus jeopardize their own economic interest.

Stanley Reed, a specialist in Middle Eastern affairs, wrote about the Arab infatuation with keeping their investments cloaked: "Why this great penchant for secrecy?" Peter Iseman, an American Arabist and repository of desert lore, says, "They never want to tell how much gold they have under the mattress."

The Arabs also sense that their great new wealth has made them enemies and perhaps increased their vulnerability. "The Saudis and Kuwaitis want people to think they are very poor," explains an executive who specializes in liaison with Arabian officials. "They want them to think they have only enough money for a few days."[1]

Muslim Influence

It is not unreasonable to expect Muslim countries to flex their economic muscles in the international political arena. In the Middle East itself, radical states such as Iran, Libya, and Syria probably will combine political and financial resources to influence the so-called moderate Arab nations. If that does not work, there is always the potential of fundamentalist Muslims trying to spark regime-toppling revolutions in the more stable Arab states, such as we have seen happen to Kuwait.

Actually, the Muslim zone of influence, far from being limited to the Middle East, is already worldwide. The use of economic-political muscle was evident in the bid for observer status for the Palestine Liberation Organization at meetings of the International Monetary Fund (IMF) and the World Bank. Such tactics had already

---

1 Peter Iseman, "Arab Investment in the U.S.," *Barron's National Business and Financial Weekly* (September 13, 1982), 8.

been used successfully by some Arab states against the IMF in 1977 when Saudi Arabia won permanent seating on the IMF Board, a step that represented a significant shift in IMF policy for Third World involvement.

Western economic dependence on oil opens the door to Arab, and therefore Islamic, influence and control. OPEC began using the oil weapon in 1973 as a punitive measure against countries that supported Israel in the Yom Kippur War. That was merely the beginning of what promises to become a master economic and political strategy, undergirded by religious conviction, for promoting Islamic interests throughout the world. Unlike the 1973 oil embargo, most of the pressures these days are subtle.

The United States is the world's largest importer of foreign oil. As much as some American economists would like to deny it, America has become dependent on a system which, to a great degree, can subject the world's strongest economy to its own desires and whims. By the mid-seventies the United States was importing an average of 8.67 million barrels of oil per day, which represented 47 percent of its oil needs. A decade earlier, imported oil comprised only 12 percent of America's daily requirements.

Through the eighties, the picture stayed basically the same. The tragedy is that the United States is still very dependent on OPEC oil—despite press attention focused on her dangerous addiction, despite the creation of a Department of Energy (which was later disassembled), and despite efforts at conservation. In 1960,

John F. Kennedy inspired the United States to soar beyond earth's gravitational pull to the moon. But three decades later, no American president has been able to successfully challenge the nation to leap out of OPEC's gravitational barrier to energy independence.

The impact of American dependence on OPEC oil has a worldwide effect. Roy Werner, assistant to United States Senator John Glenn, stated that "continuing high demand by the United States market has been a major factor in keeping OPEC prices high." In fact, following the OPEC oil embargo of 1973, and a resulting 366 percent increase in oil prices, the world energy bill rose from $20 billion in 1973 to $100 billion in 1976. That exorbitant cost dealt harshly with many of the world's major economies. There was a loss of half a million jobs and a worldwide decrease of GNP amounting to nearly $20 billion. In the nineties we are watching it happen again.

Three Islamic Convictions

To understand the relationship between OPEC and Islam, one must come to grips with the Islamic mind and three burning convictions that stem from it. The first is that economic success demonstrates God's pleasure. Prior to the development of the world's thirst for oil, Muslims measured Allah's blessing by the standards of the battlefield. Beginning with the Battle of Badr in A.D. 624, victories in war became proof of divine support.

That conviction deepened during Islam's first century as, through conquest, it spread over the Middle East, North Africa, and as far west as Spain. Since the first Arabic converts believed that Islam was the religion by which Allah revealed the weaknesses of all other faiths, they were convinced that Muslim victories validated their cause.

Today Islam interprets financial success as evidence of Allah's blessing on all Islamic advances. This explains why these so called moderate Muslims, although embarrassed by Khomeini's excesses during the Iranian revolution, would not totally disown him. Khomeini may have spoken the truth too bluntly for them, but he did speak the truth for most Muslims.

The second conviction relates to the flow of black gold. Oil is Allah's gift to Muslims so they may achieve superiority, thus proving the supremacy of Islam and enabling the subjugation of all other religions, their adherents, and the societies where they flourish. J. B. Kelly, author of *Arabia, the Gulf and the West*, noted that as a result of

> powerful sentiments of grievance and resentment against the West, the Arabs see the oil weapon as a gift sent by God to redress the balance between Christendom and Islam . . . and to fulfill the destiny which God in His infinite wisdom has ordained for those to whom He has chosen to reveal the one true faith. Extravagant though these fancies may appear to Western eyes, they are very real to those who

entertain them, and infinitely more appealing than the calmer dictates of reason.[2]

The fact that most of the OPEC oil controllers are Muslims (with some exceptions, such as Venezuela and Nigeria) brings us to the third burning conviction welding together OPEC and Islam: Arab culture is the ideal expression of Islam. "I cannot see Arab culture separate from Islamic culture," said Algeria's Ben Bella. "I honestly would not understand the meaning of Arab culture if it were not first and foremost Islamic." But the matter is deeper than that. If there is cultural imperialism related to Islam, it is the imperialism that runs so deep that the Muslims believe the Koran can be in one language only—Arabic. Translations into languages other than Arabic are not considered to be the genuine Koran, but merely interpretations.

This belief explains the anger fanatic Muslims feel when Arab countrymen adopt certain Western cultural patterns. One of the frustrations shared by the Muslim Brotherhood and the Iranian Muslim extremists was that many people in their societies adopted Western modes of dress and preferred Western styles of entertainment. The issue, in the minds of fundamentalist Muslims, had nothing to do with whether particular elements of Western lifestyle were desirable or objectionable. The important point to those Muslims was simply that Western

---

2 J. B. Kelly, "Islam Through the Looking Glass," *The Heritage Lectures* (Washington: The Heritage Foundation, 1980), 8.

cultural attire is not Arabic and only Arabic culture can be the pure expression of Islam.

This is one of many reasons Islam has no doctrine of separation of church and state. Because of close identification with one culture and the need to maintain that culture as an expression of Islam, religion and society are merged. Imam Muhammad Jawad Chirri, the leader of Detroit's Islamic Center, observed that "with the advent of Khomeini, Muslims discovered that an Islamic state is workable, a religious state is better for everybody."

Such a philosophy grows from the desire of Muhammad himself to create a society in which religion encompasses everything.

Muslim extremists demand a society controlled, pervaded, and purged by religion and established on and maintained by Arabic culture. They are willing to use every conceivable force to achieve this so-called "Divine objective."

The Dhimmi Mentality

Islamic law is the core of Islamic thought. The Muslim attitude toward non-Muslims becomes most clear in Islamic law systems. Non-Muslims do not belong to the House of Islam (*Dar al-Islam*); therefore they belong to the House of War (*Dar al-Harb*). Although interpreters of Islamic laws have disagreed on the method for implementing this law, there are only three alternatives for dealing with non-Muslims under the

Islamic legal system: (1) they must be converted; (2) they must be subjugated; or (3) they must be eliminated (except for women, children, and slaves).

Islamic law, however, distinguishes between types of non-Muslims. Christians and Jews, for example, are in different categories from the rest. Thus, some Muslim states will permit the "infidel" to enter a formal agreement or treaty that will spare the unbeliever's life and property. In that case, the non-Muslim becomes the *dhimmi* and is subjugated in various ways. According to Islamic law a *dhimmi* must wear identifiable clothing and live in a clearly marked house. He must not ride a horse or bear arms. He must yield the right-of-way to Muslims. The *dhimmi* cannot be a witness in a legal court except in matters relating to other *dhimmis*. He cannot be the guardian of a Muslim child, the owner of a Muslim slave, or a judge in a Muslim court.[3]

This concept of *dhimmi* is of great significance because fundamentalists, in interpreting the Koran and Islamic law, often take minor concepts and establish major practices affecting Islamic society and economic and political policy based on them. This *dhimmi* mentality could be the smoldering fire beneath many a relationship with Islamic purists. While Western countries view petroleum issues as having primarily an economic or political connotation, the Islamic mind is thinking *dhimmi*. Since Muslims believe Islamic superiority can

---

3 See A. S. Tritton, *The Caliphs and Their Non-Muslim Subjects* (London: Frank Cass and Company, 1970).

be demonstrated by humiliating the infidel, they must find a means for bringing the unbeliever under subjugation. Oil and money provide just the means of humiliation and subjugation. The inflation and large budget deficits that inconvenience and oppress Western nations and force them to acknowledge dependence on OPEC simply prove to the Islamic oil barons that Allah is with them and that Islamic economic policy will prevail.

The New Sword

In the twentieth century, fundamentalist Muslims see oil the same way they saw the sword in the seventh century—as a means to exert the greatest possible force on their adversaries. The linkage between OPEC and Islam follows a logical sequence: economic success is proof of God's favor; this success will result in Islamic superiority; oil gives to the Arabs an ideal world state that expresses the true culture of Islam; other religions and cultures must be subjugated; and oil has been given by Allah as the new weapon for controlling the Christian West by humiliating it. Once this is achieved, to their way of thinking at least, defeating atheism (and communism) is relatively easy.

Until those from the West who sit with the sheiks at the negotiating table understand the nature of Islam, they will not understand a fundamental and neglected component of dealing with the Middle East owners of oil. The West can flood OPEC countries with geologists, petroleum engineers, economists, and diplomats, but until such experts entertain what could happen if fundamentalist Islamic ideology were completely coupled to OPEC, their understanding of the Middle East oil picture will be only partial.

The Crisis in the Gulf

In the case of the Gulf War, given the way Muslims feel about Christians and Jews, many people are asking, Why did the Saudis allow Americans—i.e. Christians and Jews—to come to their desert?

This is easily explainable. Islamic jurisprudence allows for temporary agreement with infidels if Muslims are in a state of need. Once the need passes and Muslims become strong or no longer in need, the treaty becomes no longer binding and the Muslims can break it.

It would not be surprising if down the road the Iraqis and the Saudi Muslims get cozy again. The villain then would be the United States.

CHAPTER 3

THE BIRTH OF ISLAM

To ensure his political preeminence, Muhammad talked about rewards for those who survive war and who die in the way of God, presumably the war against non-Muslims. The real importance of this concept lies in the force and the scope of the arena in which it was applied in the post-Muhammad era.

As we examine the marriage of Islamic ideology and Arab wealth, it is essential to understand how Islam began and how it developed into an anti-Western and anti-Christian religion. Looking at this history, we will see how the story of Islam became the story of the Arab world.

Until the seventh century, when the Muslim conquest drew aside the veil of obscurity, Arabia was virtually unknown. In A.D. 610, in a cave at the foot of Mount Hira near Mecca (in what is now Saudi Arabia), a man named Ibn Abd Allah from the tribe of Quaraish had a vision. As a result, this man and his work transformed the lives of millions of people and affected significantly the history of the modern world.

According to the account of Ibn Ishaq, Muhammad's first biographer, the future prophet was fast asleep when the angel Gabriel appeared and commanded him: "Recite!"

Startled and afraid, Muhammad asked, "What shall I recite?" Immediately he felt his throat tighten as if the angel had grabbed his neck and was choking him.

"Recite!" the angel again commanded.

Muhammad again felt the angel's mighty grip.

"Recite!" the angel commanded for the third time. "Recite in the name of the Lord, the Creator who created man from a clot of blood! Recite! Your Lord is most gracious. It is he who has taught man by the pen that which he does not know."

Thus it happened that Muhammad was inspired to preach the word of Allah and that the first verses of the Koran, which literally mean "recitation," were revealed to him.

Arab Religion Before Muhammad

A great stream of caravan traders constantly passed through the Arabian peninsula, making it the commercial land-link between the Mediterranean and the Far East. Trade grew until, by the middle of the sixth century, there were three major towns in northern Arabia. Mecca was by far the most important and prosperous of these, and by Muhammad's time it was quite a bustling city.

Mecca was also a religious center. Pilgrims went there from far and wide to worship at the Kaaba, Arabia's holiest pagan shrine. The Arabs of the region had a faith rooted deeply in idolatry. For centuries they had stood aloof from every attempt by Christians from Syria and

Egypt to convert them. The nomadic Bedouin tribes living in the vast Arabian desert each worshiped a variety of its own deities and nature spirits, but some gods were revered in common. The Kaaba was the shrine ←— of these commonly acknowledged deities, all of whom Muhammad later expelled when he established the Kaaba as the central shrine of the new religion of Islam.

Two factors combined to make Arabia unusually resistant to the spread of the Christian gospel. The idolatry practiced in Mecca before the establishment of Islam was a compromise with Judaism, and it had intro- *1* duced enough legends to steel people's minds against Christianity. Also, Christianity in the seventh century was itself corrupt and decrepit, beset as it was by all *2* kinds of heresies and schisms, particularly regarding the nature of Christ. The New Testament was respected, if not revered, as a book that claimed to be the revealed Word of God, but the few Christians in Arabia had embraced a lackluster Christianity. Thus, Christianity as practiced in Arabia held no appeal for most of the people there.

The tenets of Judaism, however, were widely familiar to the Arabians through Jewish legends. To some extent, worship at the Kaaba was founded on Jewish *?* patriarchal traditions common to Christianity as well.

Thus, the ground Muhammad planted with Islam was a wide, fertile field. The potential for a great transformation of religious consciousness in Arabia was there, but it needed molding and shaping. Muhammad was the workman. Had Muhammad, stern in his early convictions, followed the leading of Christian truth, there might have been in Christian history a Saint Muhammad—more likely, Muhammad the Martyr—laying the foundation stone of the Arabian church.

Abraham and Islam

Legend attributes the building of the Kaaba to Abraham. As Hagar was wandering in the desert with her young son, Ishmael, they reached Mecca nearly dead of thirst. While Hagar was looking for water between two hills, Ishmael waited in the shade of a tree. Then, as Ishmael cried out with thirst, small bubbles under his feet became a stream of sweet, flowing water. The place where the water is believed to have first appeared is known as the well of Zemzem, which still gives water today. On a subsequent visit to Zemzem, the legend continues, Abraham was to offer his son as a sacrifice, but he was stopped by God. Abraham, assisted by his son, then built the Kaaba at God's command. However, Jews who lived in Arabia at the time refused to participate in the pagan worship at the Kaaba, refuting the story as myth by claiming that Abraham never came as far as Mecca. Now this "holy place" is the focal point of Islamic worship.

Basing his claim on the legend of the Kaaba, Muhammad sought to legitimize his new religion. He argued that Islam's relationship to Abraham made it the equal of Judaism and Christianity. Later in his life, however, he revised this claim, stating that his revelation superseded both Judaism and Christianity and had become the final revelation of God.

The Life of the Prophet

Born in Mecca in the autumn of A.D. 570, Muhammad was given his name by his mother and his grandfather. The name, rare among Arabs, means "highly praised." His father, a trader named Abdullah, died before Muhammad was born. According to the custom of Meccan aristocracy, the infant Muhammad was sent to the desert to be wet-nursed by a Bedouin mother. Muhammad spent most of his childhood years with the nurse Halima among the Beni Saad tribesmen.

At age five Muhammad was returned to his mother, but she became ill and died. His care was then the responsibility of Abdul Muttalib, his grandfather, who loved Muhammad devotedly. Unfortunately, the grandfather also soon died, and Abu Talib, Muhammad's uncle, took charge of him.

At the age of twelve, Muhammad took his first business trip to Syria with Abu Talib. It was a several-month journey filled with a multitude of rich experiences that were not wasted on Muhammad. They passed through Jewish settlements and came in contact with the Christians in Syria. No doubt he saw the churches, the crosses, and the images and symbols of their faith.

Muhammad was exposed in still another important way to the winds of religious debate blowing through the Middle East in the seventh century. At the annual fairs in Mecca, Christian as well as Jewish poets and theologians would gather to recite their poetry or preach the essence of their faith to the gathered crowds.

The influence of Judaism and Christianity on Muhammad was in form only, however, and did not give him a genuine understanding of either doctrine. Muhammad showed far more familiarity with Judaism than with Christianity, probably because Judaism was much more prominent in the area. But one thing Muhammad understood clearly was the disdainful way in which Christians and Jews regarded each other and how both spurned the Arab tribes as heathens bound to receive the wrath of an offended God.

Little else is known about Muhammad's teen years. Like other lads, he tended the sheep and goats of Mecca in the neighboring hills and valleys. Authorities agree that he was respected for his thoughtful nature and his integrity; he was nicknamed al-Amin, "the trustworthy." He must have lived a quiet, peaceful life with the family of Abu Talib.

At twenty-five, traveling the same route he had trekked thirteen years earlier with his uncle, Muhammad led a caravan expedition to Syria for a widow named Khadija. There Muhammad lost no time delving into the practices of the Syrian Christians and conversing with the monks and clergy he met. Later, in writing the Koran, he spoke of them with respect and even praise. For their doctrine, though, he had no sympathy because of his misunderstanding of the true teachings of Christ.

It is possible that the picture of Christianity in the

Koran was painted from impressions formed on this journey. It is also possible that in the sincerity of his early search after the truth, he might readily have embraced, and faithfully adhered to, the teaching of Jesus. But, as Sir William Muir said,

> Instead of the simple message of the Gospel as a revelation of God reconciling mankind unto Himself through His son, the sacred dogma of the trinity was forced upon the traveler with . . . offensive zeal . . . and the worship of Mary was exhibited in so gross a form as to leave the impression in Muhammad's mind that she was held to be a goddess if not the third person of the trinity.[1]

Add to this the ancient Arab pagan belief that the gods could have sexual intercourse with human women, producing children called the sons of God, and it is understandable that Muhammad rejected what he thought to be the Christian teaching. Far be it from the holy God to produce Jesus through sexual intercourse with a human. Thus, Muhammad refused to call Jesus the Son of God, choosing instead to call Him the son of Mary.

Upon returning from that first commercial expedition, which proved to be very successful financially, Muhammad married Khadija. She was fifteen years older

---

1 Sir William Muir, *The Life of Mohammed* (Edinburgh: John Grant, 1923), 22.

and had been married twice before. Although Muhammad would have nine other wives and other concubines after her death, he had none but Khadija while she lived. In turn, she gave him unfailing support when he began preaching to the Meccans a message they did not want to hear. She also bore Muhammad two sons and a daughter.

Muhammad Finds His Mission

As he approached forty, Muhammad spent more and more time pondering the question "What is truth?" His soul was perplexed, especially by the social injustice he saw even among the clans in his own tribe.

Muhammad's clan was the poorer group of the two main clans in the tribe of Quaraish. Naturally he was distressed to watch the rival clan grow rich and strong while his own grew weaker. One of his aims was to create a more just social system that would protect the poor, the widows, and the orphans, and would replace the existing system in which the strong abused the weak.

Thus burdened, Muhammad frequently meditated in solitude in the countryside near Mecca; a favorite spot was a cave about two or three miles to the north. One day his contemplation and search were over—the day of his disturbing and fateful vision—and he returned from his solitude and told Khadija that God had commissioned him to preach. She lost no time in consulting her *hanif* kinsman, a holy man who listened to the story and unhesitatingly declared that Muhammad had been chosen, like Moses, to receive divine inspiration and to be the prophet of his people.

The Muslims insist that Muhammad was illiterate. This, of course, substantiates his claim to have received his revelations directly from Allah. Muslims consider Muhammad's sacred vision and the subsequent recitation which make up the Koran to be miraculous acts of God. Muhammad himself, however, worked no miracles, and Islam vehemently asserts the ordinary humanity of the prophet. Muslims do not like to be called Muhammadans because it implies that they worship Muhammad as Christians worship Christ.

Even before his first revelation, Muhammad had earned a reputation for being a wise and saintly man. According to legend, Muhammad looked out from his balcony one day to see members of four clans engaged in a dispute as to who would carry the Black Stone, which the pagan Arabs regarded as sacred, to its new niche in the Kaaba. Muhammad successfully resolved the argument to everyone's satisfaction by proposing a compromise. He instructed each tribe to lift one corner of a blanket upon which he placed the meteorite, and he personally set the Black Stone in its resting place, where it remains today.

During the period following his initial revelation, Muhammad received no further messages from God, and he began to become fearful and depressed, even to the point of considering suicide. That period is thought to have lasted anywhere from six months to three years. However, the accounts are confused and sometimes contradictory. We can only conclude that there was a season during which Muhammad's mind was confused, and he was uncertain of himself and his mission.

Some unproven traditions might explain that period. Waraqa ibn Naufal, Khadija's cousin, was a Christian scholar who, we are told, translated portions of the New Testament into Hebrew and Arabic. Waraqa was tutoring Muhammad in the Christian faith, but after only a short time Waraqa died, leaving Muhammad in confusion. With no help available to relieve his frustration, Muhammad decided to go his own way alone.

Muhammad's own account of his revelation is worth noting. "Inspiration," he said,

> cometh in one of two ways; sometimes Gabriel communicateth the revelation to me, as one man to another, and this is easy; at other times, it is like the ringing of a bell, penetrating my very heart, and rending me; and this it is which afflicteth me the most.[2]

Muhammad and the Jews of Arabia

By the time he was forty-four, Muhammad had emerged from doubt and obscurity. He asserted unequivocally that he was ordained a prophet with a commission to the people of Arabia, reciting his warnings and exhortations and messages as coming directly from

2 Muir, *The Life of Mohammed.*

God. He taught that Allah was the one God and that men must thank him for their existence and worship him only. He preached equality before God and justice among men and warned that because man's destiny was in God's hands, there would be a Day of Judgment for all men. His wife Khadija was his first convert, followed by his slave Zaid, whom he later adopted as his son. Then followed two of his most trusted friends, Abu Bakr and Umar, who later succeeded him as leaders of the Muslim movement. But in Mecca, Muhammad met with stiff opposition from his own tribe; they refused to acknowledge him as a prophet and refused to give up idol worship.

During the early years of his mission, Muhammad developed a close relationship with the Jews. Some acknowledged him to be the prophet, the messiah, descended from Abraham. The majority of Jews, however, maintained a "wait and see" policy. Muhammad, in turn, incorporated into the new religion many Jewish traditions and numerous Old Testament stories. Those include, as we saw earlier, the story of Abraham and Isaac, the story of Hagar and Ishmael, stories about Joseph and Jacob, and the account of the destruction of Sodom and Gomorrah. In the Koran, those stories are usually mixed with other extrabiblical incidents.

Muhammad's attempt to turn the hearts of the Meccans proved frustrating and unsuccessful. Mecca enjoyed a religious society that was closely connected with its commercial activity, and it proved to be a closed society that Muhammad was unable to penetrate.

Discouraged, Muhammad and his followers went to

the city of Medina in a mass migration known in Islamic history as the *hijra*. In Medina, Muhammad struck a much more responsive chord in the people's hearts. The city harbored a large community of Jews who endlessly threatened the pagans with warnings that the coming Messiah would revenge the injustice inflicted upon them. This situation made the population ready to accept Muhammad's message, and they were more prepared for monotheistic religious ideas than were the worldly Meccans.

That sociopolitical arrangement provided Muhammad with the perfect opportunity to bring Jews and pagans together under the banner of Allah. In doing so, he tried to please the Jews by adopting some of their religious rites. The Jewish Day of Atonement became the Muslim fast day of Ashura. Prayer was increased from two to three times (later to five times) daily to accommodate the Jewish midday prayer. Muslims held a public service, such as the Jews had in synagogues, with Friday equal to the Jewish sabbath. Muhammad also adopted the Jewish call to prayer, but instead of the trumpet of the Jews, Muhammad used a human prayer-caller (*muezzin*). Consequently, when disputes with the Jews occurred, their opposition and rejection of his message disappointed and angered Muhammad. He, in turn, accused the Jews of rejecting the truth and claimed Jewish property for his own private ownership.

Muhammad never seemed to show the same interest in the Christian faith. Nor did he have the same opportunity to learn its history and doctrines. However, his attitude toward Christianity was just as favorable as it had been toward Judaism. At no time was his dialogue with Christians embittered by causes similar to those that eventually led to his hostile relationship with the Jews. But Muhammad's relationship with the Christian faith never advanced significantly beyond the point at which it is described in the Koran.

Muhammad's mission followed a pattern of development that might be called "progressive revelation." He started out to warn and reform the pagan society of the Arabian peninsula, asking people to turn to the true God, the God of Abraham. Then, equating his revelation with that of Judaism and Christianity, he perceived himself to be on equal footing with Moses and Jesus. Finally, he saw himself and his message as the final word of God that superseded both previous religions.

This progression brought him to believe that Islam was the universal faith, the faith that started with Abraham (the first Muslim according to Muhammad). Muhammad believed, because Jews and Christians had moved away from God's intended purpose, that God had sent him to proclaim the ultimate revelation. In his own mind at least, Muhammad rose triumphant over both the Law and the Gospel. The new message of Allah was announced in the Arabic language and intended for Arabs, who henceforth would have a prophet and a holy book of their own.

To Muhammad, the Jew was to follow the Law and the Christian was to hold fast to the Gospel. Both Jew and Christian were to admit as equal with their own prophets and Scriptures the apostleship of Muhammad and the authority of the Koran.

> Say: O People of the Book! Ye do not stand upon any sure ground until you observe both the Torah and the Gospel as well as that which has been now sent down unto you from your Lord (the Koran, 5:68).

For a short time the Jews remained on cordial terms with their new ally. But it soon became evident that Judaism could not go hand-in-hand with Islam because Muhammad began to see his mission as more than mere protest against error and superstition. Every day Islam moved closer to being exclusive and demanding a priority status. Ultimately, at his farewell pilgrimage, Muhammad barred Christians and Jews from visiting the Kaaba and by "divine command" declared their continued exclusion until they confessed the supremacy of Islam or consented to pay tribute. "Paradise is the reward for those who die in the way of God," he declared, "and the booty is the reward of those who survive the war."

Although no one can deny the significance of Muhammad's religious conviction, it is evident that Muhammad, in addition to espousing a doctrine, formed a new religious society. To ensure his political preeminence, he talked about rewards for those who survive war and who die in the way of God, presumably the war against non-Muslims. The real importance of this concept lies in the force and the scope of the arena in which it was applied in the post-Muhammad era.

Throughout the Koran, Muhammad developed a form of theocratic government pertinent to all departments of life, beginning with the conduct of dissidents, the treatment of allies, the formation of treaties, and other political matters. Later, elements of a code of conduct and moral law were introduced.

Few men have had such impact on the world as Muhammad. Thirteen centuries after his death, about 700 million people are followers of the religion he founded.

Toward the end of his life, Muhammad began to clarify his own aspirations as to the future spread of Islam. He made a silver seal engraved with the words "Muhammad the apostle of God" and sent four simultaneous messages bearing this stamp to the rulers of Egypt, Abyssinia, Syria, and Persia, urging them to forsake their idols and to believe the true universal faith of God's message given through him, God's messenger.

When Muhammad was sixty-three, and Islam was only twenty years old, the "apostle of God" fell ill with a sudden fever and died. As the news of his death spread, the new Muslims were seized with panic and confusion. But Abu Bakr, Muhammad's close friend and later the first Islamic caliph (successor of the Prophet), declared to Muhammad's distraught followers, "Whichever of you worships Muhammad, know that Muhammad is dead. But which of you worships God, know that God is alive and does not die." He then quoted a verse from the Koran which gains significance with the hindsight of history: "Muhammad is a Prophet only; there have been Prophets before him. If he dies or is slain, will ye turn back?"

Holy War

Even this brief sketch of the spiritual and historical roots of Islam is sufficient to illustrate one of Islam's most powerful concepts, that of *jihad*, "holy war." The word literally means "struggle." Not every Muslim would agree that *jihad* requires spilling the blood of infidels, but the struggle for the victory of Islam is a factor in the life of every faithful Muslim.

Al-Banna explained the importance of *jihad* this way:

> How wise was the man who said "force is the surest way of implementing the right and how beautiful it is that force and right should march side by side." This striving to broadcast the Islamic mission, quite apart from preserving the hallowed concepts of Islam, is another re-ligious duty imposed by God on the Muslims, just as he imposed fasting, prayer, pilgrimage, alms, and the doing of good and abandonment of evil, upon them. He imposes it upon them and delegated them to do it. He did not excuse anyone possessing strength and capacity from performing it. . . .[3]

Jihad, according to Islamic law, is to be waged until

3 Hasan Al-Banna, "To What Do We Summon Mankind?" *Five Tracts of Hasan Al-Banna*, trans. Charles Wendell (Berkeley: University of California Press, 1978), 80.

the Day of Judgment—or forever. There may be times when Muslim armies appear to be defeated, but even legal armistices can be broken when in the best interests of Islam. But there can be no possible permanent peaceful equality with infidels. Since superiority is such a vital factor in Islamic thought, domination is the only worthy expression of Islam's greatness.

It is not strange, therefore, to read in the Koran that Allah exhorts Muslims to not take Jews or Christians for friends:

> Oh ye who believe! Take not the Jews and Christians for friends. They are friends one to another. He among you who taketh them for friends is one of them (5:51).

This theme is repeated again in the Koran:

> Believers do not make friends with anyone other than your own people. They desire nothing but ruin. Their hatred is clear from what they say, but more violent is the hatred which their breasts conceal (3:118).

According to Muslim extremists, such Koranic texts as the one quoted above enforce this intolerant attitude toward non-Muslims. They also constantly exhort the "faithful" to begin a holy war against Jews, Christians, and other non-Muslims. This teaching may communicate that it is virtually impossible for Muslims to interact on a trust basis with anyone who is not a member of the Muslim brotherhood. I have, however, known Muslims who feel that these texts were for certain historical periods and that they are not binding upon them today.

Islamic "superiority" reaches its apex in the Koran in chapter 5, verse 33. There, Muslims are commanded to fight non-Muslims and anyone who rejects Allah and his apostle (Muhammad). How are they to deal with the enemy? By crucifying them, or cutting off their hands and feet on alternate sides, or banishing them from the country.

Generally speaking, Muslim *jihad* is no longer waged by the sword (although isolated incidents such as the assassination of President Anwar Sadat of Egypt fit that description). The imperative to subjugate non-Muslims, however, remains an essential ingredient of the love of Islamic philosophy, justifying and even demanding the use of any extremity of power to accomplish that purpose.

Only the outer form of *jihad* has changed, not the inner reality. Today, economic *jihad* is the major strategy of some Islamic states. What can stand in the way of the tremendous growth of Arab oil wealth and the power it is capable of wielding?

CHAPTER 4

CONTRASTS BETWEEN CHRISTIAN AND ISLAMIC THEOLOGY

In the effort to accord Allah all the honor his power deserves, Islam has seriously underestimated the real power of God. Muslims simply are unable to comprehend the tremendous power of divine love that chose to live humbly as a man among men so that all might know God.

*T*here is no god but God, and Muhammad is the Messenger of God." This confession of faith, a brief eight words in Arabic, sums up the central belief of the world's Muslims. It also establishes the common ground between Islam and other religions that proclaims the existence of a sovereign God who makes himself known to humankind. Like Judaism and Christianity, the older religions that preceded and influenced it, Islam is both a monotheistic and revealed religion (in other words, its followers believe it came by direct revelation from God).

Although the Islamic concept of God appears similar in some respects to the Judeo-Christian concept, it is also different in several important ways.

As we deal with the Muslim world, we need to know some of the fundamental principles of their seemingly similar, but actually very different, religion. Knowing them—and how they vary from biblical doctrine—we can better understand what motivates Muslims to wage and win an ongoing holy war.

Monotheism was the conviction of the prophet Muhammad, and belief in one God is the pivot on which Islamic doctrine revolves. The Koran does not attempt to prove or argue the existence of Allah; it proclaims his existence as a matter of fact. The word Islam itself means "submission to God"—nothing less than the total surrender of man's life to the all-knowing, all-powerful Allah.

Furthermore, Muslims believe God has spoken to man through the prophets, particularly the prophet Muhammad, who Muslims regard as the final prophet of God. Although Islam acknowledges other prophets before Muhammad's time—the great figures of the Old and New Testaments such as Abraham, Moses, David, and Jesus—Muslims believe God gave Muhammad the complete revelation of the final divine truth. Thus ultimate knowledge of God can be found only through the pages of the Koran, the collection of Muhammad's proclamations, which his followers memorized and recorded, in which Allah allegedly made known his laws and spelled out what he expects from man morally, ethically, and religiously.

Muslim sacred scripture is emphatic in asserting that since Allah has made his will clearly known in the Koran, man has no alternative but to obey it literally. The same enormous zeal with which the Koran bears witness to God is evident today in the lives and actions of those Muslims who believe Islam has lost its original fervor because of compromise with Western godlessness.

Man's objective in life, according to Muslim teaching, should be a true knowledge of Allah's word as revealed in the Koran, and a total submission to his will. The enforcement of what is perceived to be God's law on earth is of paramount importance to zealous Muslims, as demonstrated in the fanatical pursuit of this goal in Egypt, Pakistan, Syria, and Iran. The assassins of President Sadat declared that they had upheld Islam's teachings by killing a man whom they thought to be compromising the Islamic religion. And the Ayatollah Khomeini did not spare the lives of some of his closest friends when they disagreed with his convictions about what form an Islamic government should take to satisfy Koranic demands.

The phenomenon of religious persecution raises disturbing questions about the relationship between Islam and its "sister" religions, especially Christianity. Are Muslim fanatics correctly interpreting the directives of the Koran when they subjugate non-Muslims? If so, doesn't the Koran contradict the Bible? And if that is so, how can they both be revelations of one God? Yet Muslims claim to worship the same God Christians do. Obviously, both religions have traveled a long way down different roads since they met and agreed on monotheism and revelation.

Where Christianity and Islam Differ

As mentioned earlier, on the surface there is a great deal of resemblance between the Islamic view of God, or

Allah, and the God of Judeo-Christian tradition. The Koran gives ninety-nine attributes of God, or "most Beautiful Names," with which Christians would agree; among these is that Allah is the All-Powerful, the Creator, the Merciful, and the Compassionate.

This apparent agreement is misleading, however. It is a mistake to assume that Muslims and Christians perceive God basically in the same manner just because they describe him in similar terms. On a deeper level, the differences between Muslim and Christian understandings of how people should relate to God and to others are even greater.

In the final analysis, the Christian perception of God and response to him make the crucial difference in the lives of the committed Christians. Both Islam and Christianity accept by faith what they assert has been revealed to them by God; yet their claims to divine truth rival each other just as their prescriptions for living do. "By their fruit you will recognize them," Jesus said in Matthew 7:20, reiterating an age-old truth of human nature: a person's behavior is the most convincing demonstration of his or her understanding of God.

Consider the phenomenon of religious persecution. Certainly the behavior of many professing Christians indicates they are not immune to self-righteousness, prejudice, hatred, and all the other ills of common humanity. But there is nothing in Christianity that condones, much less endorses, such attitudes and behavior. Quite the contrary, the true Christian constantly strives, with the help of God, to weed from life anything that hinders the growth of love. For the genuine Christian, the self-giving love of God revealed in Jesus Christ is the same love the Christian is called upon to show toward others. Jesus' clear instruction to his followers was, "Love each another as I have loved you" (John 15:12).

Christians always have fallen short of the ideal imitation of Christ, and the history of Christianity is filled with spectacular examples of such failure. The Crusades, the Spanish Inquisition of the Middle Ages, and the vicious extremism of contemporary Northern Ireland are among Christianity's most shameful examples of misguided zeal. But the practitioners of such distortions, the "Christian" extremists, violate their own professed faith. Although Christianity acknowledges and understands human weakness and the persistent tendency to turn against one's neighbor, it considers acts of religious persecution by its own adherents to be ignorant and evil perversions of the love of Christ.

The same is not true of Islam. Judgmentalism is at the core of Islamic fundamentalism, and nothing within it restrains or counters the human temptation to judge and condemn others. This includes fellow Muslims whom fundamentalists perceive as compromisers. While Christianity, despite mistakes and even atrocities committed in its name, remains essentially a faith of love, forgiveness, and new life, Islam is a religion of law, submission, and punishment. The concept "Do not judge, or you too will be judged" (Matthew 7:1) is foreign to fundamentalist Muslim thought.

The most striking theological focus of the differences between the two religions is the Christian doctrine of the Incarnation, which Islam flatly rejects. The problem seems to have its source in Muhammad's original misunderstanding of the Christian concept of the Son of God. Christians believe that the Son is none other than God in the flesh, having taken human form.

Muhammad, however, influenced by the polytheistic environment of pre-Islamic Arabia, thought Christians believed that God "married" and produced a son. To Muhammad, very rightly, that was a pagan belief. Furthermore, Muhammad also mistakenly thought Christians believed that the Trinity consists of Jesus, God, and Mary. Considering the various heresies surrounding the worship of Mary at the time of Muhammad's interest in Christianity, it is not too difficult to imagine how he arrived at the erroneous conclusion that Christians worship more than one God.

Muslims regard Jesus as a prophet of God, and they accept his miracles. But Muslims believe that Christian faith in the divinity of Jesus is polytheism. Consequently, although Christians have special status in Islam as "People of the Book," Muslims believe that the Bible in its present form is corrupt and that only the Koran contains the ultimate truth. Thus, to some extent, Islam arose out of a misunderstanding of Christianity—a crucial misunderstanding in view of the tremendous implications it carries.

When Muslims reject the concept of God-become-man, they also reject the concept of a relationship between God and man, which is the essence of Christian faith. Put simply, Islam delineates a concept of God that ultimately is irreconcilable with the Christian Gospel. Muslims do not believe that God would have an interest in a personal relationship of love and friendship with man, much less that he actually would enter into human history for the purpose of establishing, or rather re-establishing, such a relationship.

But Christians affirm that this is precisely the meaning of Jesus' life, death, and resurrection. Jesus said to his disciples, "I no longer call you servants. . . . Instead I have called you friends" (John 15:15). The Christian Gospel emphasizes God's offer of intimate friendship with man—the possibility of loving communion with God. Islam put exclusive and legalistic emphasis on some of the commandments of God.

According to Muslims, divinity and humanity are totally exclusive entities. They believe God really could not have entered into human life and that the relationship with God enjoyed by Christians is impossible. Fellowship with God, which is the religious experience of the Christian, is unimaginable to Muslims. They consider the Christian assertion that man was created in God's own image to be blasphemous.

The careful reader of the Koran cannot escape the impression that the essence of Allah is power—power overrides all his other attributes. The Creation itself was an act of Allah's absolute power, an expression of his might as lord reigning over all worlds and kingdoms. God's eternal power is clearly demonstrated in the Creation, as the Koran testifies:

> See they not the clouds, how they are created?
> And the heaven, how it is raised high and the
> mountains, how they are fixed and the earth,
> how it is spread out? (88:17–20).

In contrast, man is "servant" to his "master," God. God decrees everything that happens, and man has no real choice but to submit to the divine will. Allah's power, of itself, qualifies him to act as arbitrarily as he pleases. According to the Koran, "He leads and misleads whom he will" (74:34).

Furthermore, the Koran goes so far as to say that humans have little choice in determining the purpose of their lives:

> Man does not enter the world or leave it as he
> desires. He is a creature; and the Creator, who
> has brought him into existence and bestowed
> upon him higher and more excellent faculties
> than upon other animals, has also assigned an
> object to his existence (15:29).

Some of this may sound similar to the Bible, but in the Koran the image of the sovereign God is not tempered by a loving, compassionate side. The Koran stresses the concept that by God's design humans should devote all their faculties to the practice of religion:

> Therefore stand firm in your devotion to the
> true faith, which Allah himself has made and
> for which he has made men (30:30).

The Koran relates that God created man from the "crackling clay of black mud" and then breathed into him the breath of life:

> He formed and fashioned the body of Adam from the dry clay and then he breathed into the body of his own spirit; and man, an embodied soul, came into being (15:28, 29).

On the surface, the Koran parallels the biblical account of creation. It stresses, however, the idea that man is God's viceroy, his substitute on earth. It does not attach particular significance to the story of man's fall from communion with God. There are two reasons for that: Muslims do not believe in man's original communion with God as the purpose for which he was created, and they do not believe in original sin.

The Koranic view of the nature of man can be expressed this way: Man was created good; in fact, his nature is superior to the angelic hosts themselves, who were commanded to bow down before him at his creation. But being mortal, man is inconstant when tested with evil. He fell through the temptation of Satan, and he lost paradise, but he is not radically estranged from God. Man is prone to sin, but his basic nature is not sinful.

Christians believe that at the Fall something radical happened to man's nature. Man became totally sinful, alienated from God, and incapable of reconciliation with God through human efforts. Christians also believe that the whole purpose of existence is to live in relationship with a loving God—the relationship for which we were originally created but which sin destroyed. Therefore salvation is necessary, and the redemption Jesus Christ effected is both the restoration and the fulfillment of our reason for being.

That concept is precisely what Islam would deny. Muslims do not see man as totally sinful and incapable of saving himself. Muslims also see a totally different relationship between man and God and, accordingly, cannot understand that man was created in God's image, or that God became man.

Sin and Sinfulness

Much of what the Koran says about the practice of sin sounds, again, very much like the Bible. For example, the Koran has several words for sin, but behind all of them is the idea of failure to come up to the standards set by God. Man was created for the service of Allah, and he is supposed to obey what Allah has commanded. The root of sin lies in prideful opposition to God's will. Man is prone to wrong actions due to weakness; therefore, the only way to avoid evil is by doing good works according to God's commands. The Koran teaches that "Surely good deeds take away evil deeds" (11:114).

But the Koran does not consider sin to have tainted the nature of humanity, and thus Islam has no overall doctrine of sin. The Koran reveals that Muhammad himself had no deep conviction concerning sin, and he did not demand that believers experience any such conviction. Rather, Islam puts forth ideas about specific wrong-

CONTRASTS BETWEEN CHRISTIAN AND ISLAMIC THEOLOGY

doing to classify them as great or small for determining
the degree of punishment.

Kabira ("great sins") include things such as murder
or adultery, disobeying God or one's parents, drinking
to excess, practicing usury, neglecting Friday prayers
and the feast of Ramadan, forgetting the Koran after
reading it, swearing falsely or by any other name than
that of God, performing magic, gambling, dancing, or
shaving the beard. Such sins can be forgiven only after
repentance.

Saghira ("little sins") include lying, deception,
anger, and lust. Sins of this class are easily forgiven if the
greater sins are avoided and if some good actions are
performed.

The sin that surpasses all others is *shirk*, the association of other deities with Allah. That is unpardonable.
Tradition has it that when Muhammad was asked to
identify the greatest sin, he said it was polytheism, the
worship of more than one deity. (This, incidentally, is all
the justification Muslims would need to wage a holy war
on non-Muslims—to convert, conquer, or eliminate them
as unbelievers who have corrupted the true faith of
Allah.)

The Muslim's view of God is that of an elderly,
cherubic Arab who is always happy when people obey
him and furiously angry when they disobey—and he
rewards or punishes them accordingly. To the faithful,
he is Lord of Bounty, but like a benevolent dictator, he
insists on compliance with his laws. That is why, with
few exceptions (Turkey being one), we find few real

democracies in Islamic countries. Muslims' view of God is tied up with their view of their ruler, whether he be a monarch or a dictator.

Yet Muslims believe Allah can be merciful if he chooses. He accepts repentance and forgives faults and shortcomings. The opening words of each chapter of the Koran read, "In the name of God, the merciful." Muslims believe that every word and every accent in the Koran reveal the mercies of God.

The Koran teaches that forgiveness has to be sought because God is all-knowing (another similarity with the Bible). He sees the secrets of our lives; nothing we do escapes his notice. Allah's *maghfera* ("forgiveness") preserves a person from being touched by punishment. That Allah forgives sins is repeatedly proclaimed in the Koran, but it is important to remember that forgiveness is purely the prerogative of Allah. There is no atoning blood of Christ to cover the sins of the believer once and for all. Even though he is addressed as "merciful," Allah remains a stern, unbending God.

The Five Pillars

The five pillars of Islam summarize the Muslim's fundamental religious duties and beliefs: (1) reciting the *shahada* ("profession of faith"); (2) praying five times daily; (3) paying the *zakat* ("alms-tax"); (4) fasting and praying during the month of Ramadan; and (5) making the pilgrimage to Mecca at least once in a lifetime if financially able. These are the minimal obligations that every good Muslim must observe. They alone are not adequate to ensure that one is living a virtuous life, but they are the prerequisites of virtue.

So we see that the major emphasis in Islam is on the acts a believer performs rather than on the attitude of the believer's heart. One gains God's favor by what one does; one is not loved by God simply for who one is.

This emphasis on salvation by works rather than by faith produces anxiety for thoughtful Muslims. It is never possible to be assured that actions have earned an acquittal before the eternal Judge. The Muslim must be vigilant constantly, exercising alertness mixed with fear.

The insecurity of salvation and fear of God that are integral to Islam make it both defensive and aggressive, especially in dealing with non-Muslims. Just as sin is not essential to the nature of man in the Muslim view, neither is forgiveness essential to the nature of Allah. Allah is not bound by his own nature to forgive man. It is something he chooses to do somewhat consistently, but there is no guarantee that he will do so in every instance. There is no doubt as to what Allah expects a person to do in this life if the person is to have any hope of being admitted to paradise in the next. Nevertheless, no Muslim, no matter how devout and pious, can be sure of winning Allah's favor. Muslims pray to a God they must cajole and beg for forgiveness, and they must bow before a God unwilling to give any assurance that the sinner is forgiven.

Love and Weakness

The concept of love as one of God's attributes is conspicuously missing from Islam because in Islamic thought love is a sign of weakness. Far be it from Allah, the all-powerful, to be weak. To love is to be vulnerable, and far be it from Allah to be vulnerable. But love also produces genuine confidence and hope and teaches the beloved to love freely and generously in return. Islam has no concept of the strength of love or of the characteristic qualities of love as desirable. The Koran gives no knowledge of the perfect love of God in Jesus Christ, which casts out fear and which is strong enough to overcome death and inaugurate eternal life. Muslims cannot rest in the promise of a faithful god who assures that nothing will separate them from the love of God in Jesus Christ.

In Islam, God and man are wary of each other, in contrast to Christianity, in which God and man are in love with each other. This difference is of great importance because it lies at the heart of the tensions Muslims feel toward Christians. The same relationship that exists between God and humans in each of the two religions exists by extension between the humans. Christians are taught to love their neighbors as they have first experienced Christ's love. Muslims are taught—many exhortations to charity notwithstanding—to judge, condemn, and even eliminate their neighbors if they fail to measure up to a certain standard of faith and practice, because that is how they expect Allah to deal with them.

Islam and the Cross

The concept of the cross of Jesus Christ eludes Muslims because they do not understand the need for it. Islam cannot acknowledge the truth of the cross because it cannot see it in the first place. Furthermore, substitutionary atonement is to the Muslim mind a primitive and savage idea. Not in the shedding of blood itself, but in the fact that someone would die for someone else. Muslims cannot comprehend what to Christians is the highest kind of love—a love that takes the consequences of sin upon itself and finds its meaning in forgiveness and redemption.

And yet the cross can be present in Islam, too, even if unrecognized. It is ironic, and an affirmation of the mysterious workings of God's grace, that Muslims are required by the Koran to read the *Injeil*, or Christian Gospel, for the value of its moral teaching, even though they reject its most basic message. All Christians should pray sincerely that Muslims genuinely will be instructed by the truth hidden deep within the mandate of their own religion, waiting for them to discover its divine riches. For Christ was speaking to all people when he said, "You will know the truth, and the truth will set you free" (John 8:32).

The Day of Judgment

The reality and importance of the Day of Judgment in Islam is second only to the reality and importance of

Allah himself. The Koran employs some of its most striking language to describe "the event which will overwhelm mankind," when the earth and human society will be destroyed, the dead will be resurrected, and every soul will stand before God to be judged and assigned to dwell for eternity in heaven or hell.

> We moulded man into a most noble image and in the end We shall reduce him to the lowest of the low, except the believers who do good works, for theirs shall be a boundless recompense. What, then can after this make you deny the Last Judgment? Is Allah not the best of judges? (95:4–8)

The God of Islam is not only the benevolent Creator who generously lavishes on mankind all earthly blessings, but also the vengeful Judge who, having demanded submission to his divine will, mercilessly imposes inevitable and terrible punishment on those who spurn him and transgress his laws. This stands in stark contrast to Christianity's loving God, who, even as he judges in righteousness, is "patient with you, not wanting anyone to perish" (2 Peter 3:9).

To be a Muslim is to believe in God, the prophecy of Muhammad, and the Last Judgment. But because Islam is a blend in equal proportions of spiritual beliefs and concrete rules of conduct, to be a Muslim is also to live in a specifically prescribed way. Not to do so practically guarantees damnation to unending torment. Thus, in Islam the underlying motivation for faith is fear.

The Koran further teaches that man's hour of death is ordained:

> When their doom comes, they are not able to delay it an hour, nor can they advance it (16:61).

Muslims believe that Allah decrees everything that happens, including a person's entrance into this world and death, which ushers him into the next. Birth and death are merely two aspects of the phenomenon of life that Allah owns and controls.

The irrevocable finality of death is also very clearly spelled out in the Koran. When someone begs Allah to return him to earth, the answer comes:

> By no means! It is but a word that he speaks and before them is a barrier, until the day they are raised (23:100).

Only Allah knows exactly when the Last Judgment will come.

> They ask then about the hour when will it come to pass? Say: The knowledge thereof is with my Lord only (7:187).

But there is no doubt in the Koran concerning the reality of the day of judgment. It is expected of a Muslim to believe in that reality, almost in the same way he believes in God. Again, this teaching is much like Christian thought on the subject.

In Islam, the hereafter is divided into heaven and

hell. In heaven, believers will experience God's favor and benevolence. In hell, unbelievers will experience God's severity and wrath.

The Koran describes both places in vivid terms. Heaven is an oasis-paradise filled with "gardens watered by running streams," rivers of milk, wine, clarified honey, and shade trees bearing all kinds of fruits.

In hell, on the other hand, people will be made to drink boiling water, molten metal, and decaying filth. "Then as for those who are unhappy, they will be in the fire; for them there will be sighing and groaning" (11:106). Hell has seven divisions, each with its particular purpose and terrors for various heretics and unbelievers. There is a Muslim purgatory, a special division of hell for Christians, one for Jews, and a bottomless pit for hypocrites. Obviously, many of these details are at odds with biblical teaching.

As for the Last Judgment itself, the clearest and most concise description of the Muslim's view is found in L. Bevan Jones's book, *The People of the Mosque*.[1] He divided the events of the Last Day into what he called "the four outstanding features."

According to Muslim tradition, the Last Day will not come until there is no one found who calls on God. Then "the sounding of the trumpet" will signal the arrival of the Day of Judgment. At the first blast of the trumpet, everyone in heaven and earth will die except those

---

1 L. Bevan Jones, *The People of The Mosque* (Calcutta: Associated Press, YMCA, 1932).

whom God saves. At the second trumpet blast, the dead will be resurrected.

After the resurrection, there will follow a period of forty years when people will wander about the earth naked, confused, and sorrowful. They must await "the descent of the books," which have been kept by the recording angels. Each book will be given to its owner, delivered into the right hand of those who are good, and into the left hand of those who are wicked. Next "the scales" will weigh each one's good and bad deeds, and their fate will be determined. The good deeds are heavy; the bad deeds are light. Prophets and angels will be exempt from this trial, and according to some authorities, so will believers. ? so why ple anxiety

Finally, when the preceding tests have been concluded, everyone will have to cross "the bridge," a very narrow road "sharper than the edge of a sword, finer than a hair, suspended over hell" (36:66). Those who are to be saved will pass over it quickly, but those who are condemned will fall into hell and remain there forever.

Jesus and the Muslim's Day of Judgment

As for knowing when the Last Day is approaching, one of the most popular beliefs among Muslims is that Jesus will return, declare himself a Muslim, and will call the world to Islam. Then he will die a normal death. Muslims believe that when the Roman soldiers came to Jesus at night, before they laid hands on him, God pulled him up to heaven. The return of Jesus is one of the

Jesus didn't die

definitive signs of the Last Day, in Muslim thinking, presumably because of their belief that Jesus did not die but was lifted up to heaven before the Crucifixion. It is not difficult to see that Islam has adopted only partial segments of the teaching of the New Testament.

The harshness of Islam is the direct result of its uncertainty about salvation and eternity. Not only are people what they worship, but they become what they fear. The Muslim's fear of Allah's judgment and condemnation turns outward into the same kind of action toward others. Grace and forgiveness are rare attributes of God or man in Islam, which proves a common saying that "Islam is as arid as the deserts of its birth."

Islam has failed to perceive accurately God's declared purpose for man, or why God is interested in man at all. Muslims bend over backward paying homage to the power of God out of the erroneous belief that God is mainly concerned with exacting tribute. In this regard Islam is curiously like the pre-Islamic tribal religions it so strenuously rejected. One reason Christ's coming was necessary, Christians believe, was that, at the time of Jesus, Judaism had become such a distortedly legalistic religion. The Jews did not understand that God was much more interested in the inward attitude of the believer's heart than in the outward show of religion. Islam is similar to Judaism in that respect.

The tragedy of Islam is, because it does not recognize God's real concern for reestablishing a relationship of love with mankind, that Muslims deprive themselves of the joy of participating in that relationship. Paradoxically, in the effort to accord Allah all the honor his power deserves, Islam has seriously underestimated the real power of God. Muslims simply are unable to comprehend the tremendous power of divine love that chose to live humbly as a man among men so that all might know God.

Love WINS!

CHAPTER 5

SUNNI–SHIITE DIVISION

The current instability in the governments of the Middle East grows out of several long-standing disputes in the Arab Muslim world over such issues as fundamentalism versus secularism, politics versus religion, and the Sunni branch of Islam versus the Shiite branch.

*I*n October 1981, Iranian pilgrims bound for Mecca were deported by Saudi troops for carrying Khomeini's posters and tracts calling for the overthrow of the Saudi regime. In December of the same year, another event shocked the Middle East. A group of Shiite Muslims from several Arab states tried unsuccessfully to overthrow Bahrain's Sunni government. And in August 1990 Iraq's dictator, Saddam Hussein, invaded neighboring Kuwait.

The current instability in the governments of the Middle East grows out of several long-standing disputes in the Arab Muslim world over such issues as fundamentalism versus secularism, politics versus religion, and the Sunni branch of Islam versus the Shiite branch. The last of these disputes is especially relevant to the current crisis and poses particular threats to economic and other interests of the West.

The Iran-Iraq war widened the old divisions within Islam. But as the Gulf Crisis became the Gulf War, the people of Iran and the Iraqi military state openly decried the presence of American troops on Islamic soil. Iraqis had previously perceived that Khomeini in Iran was trying to increase the importance of his Shiite sect of Islam at the expense of all the others.

Perhaps a way to explain the differences between the sects in Islam would be to compare them to the different denominations of Christianity. During the Protestant Reformation there was a split in the Christian church and Protestants left the dominant branch of Christianity, the Roman Catholic church. Following the Reformation, the Protestants split into several branches.

Something similar happened in Islam. After the death of Ali, the fourth caliph (successor to Muhammad), Islam split into two groups. The splinter group (the followers of Ali) then split again. Khomeini was the leader of one of these splinter sects, Twelver Shiite Islam.

A Brief History of Shiism

Following the death of Muhammad, his trusted friend Abu Bakr was named the first caliph. Abu Bakr was one of the first converts to Islam, Muhammad's close advisor, and also his father-in-law. The choice of Abu Bakr to lead the newly founded Islamic *Ummah* ("community of believers") disappointed Ali (Muhammad's cousin, son-in-law, and close friend). Ali, considering himself Muhammad's legitimate heir and successor, thought he should have been named caliph. Only after two more successors, Umar and Othman, had died in power did Ali become caliph. Following his ascension a power struggle ensued and Ali was assassinated by Muawiya (founder of the Umayyad Dynasty). The caliphate passed on to the monarchical House of Umayyad. However, Ali's son, Hussein, claimed that as Muhammad's grandson the caliphate belonged to him. The struggle that followed split the Muslim world into supporters of the House of Ali and supporters of the House of Umayyad. Hussein was killed in a battle with Caliph Yazid of the Umayyads. The split became permanent with his death. The two main groups being the *Shi-at Ali* (the party of Ali), supporting the descendants of Ali as rightful rulers, and the Sunni (the followers of the Prophet's Path), supporting first the Umayyads and then the Abbasids.

Defeated by the Sunnis, the Shiites felt a deep sense of having been wronged:

> They became dissenters, subversives within the Arab empire, given to violence against authority. Shiite Islam was an extremely emotional sect and still is. Its adherents at times clothe themselves in black cloaks and black turbans, and once a year reenact the passion of Husayn (Hussein), sometimes flagellating themselves as a means of atoning for Husayn's (Hussein's) martyrdom.[1]

---

1 James Cook, "Sunnis? Shiites? What's That Got To Do With Oil Prices?" *Forbes* (April 12, 1982), 99.

Shiites insist that the descendants of Ali are the *Imams* ("leaders"). Imams are considered to be sinless, almost infallible leaders in all spheres of life, including politics. They also are able to interpret and reinterpret the Koran. Shiites believe in a continuing revelation of God's word through the Imams.

The Twelver Shiite sect of Khomeini teaches that the infant Twelfth Imam went into hiding in the ninth century and will remain hidden until the end of time, when he will return to earth as the *Mahdi* ("Messiah") to establish the millennium of perfect equity.

Twelver Shiites believe that until the Twelfth Imam returns, every true Muslim must put himself under the authority of a holy man—an ayatollah. This belief has given rise to a strong clergy and a religious hierarchy. From those men alone can salvation come. They also wield enormous secular power.

Early in the sixteenth century, Twelver Shiism was made the official religion of Persia (now called Iran). The clergy became increasingly powerful. In other Muslim countries Sunni religious authorities were absorbed into the state; they became part of the civil service in Egypt. The Shiite clergy, on the other hand, developed a tradition of opposition to the state. They believed that the state owed religious obedience to them. In 1906 the Shiite clergy in Persia led the revolution that established a constitution and caused the fall of the two-hundred-year-old Qajar dynasty. They caused the rise of the first Pahlavi Shah, Reza Shah, and the fall of the second, Muhammad Shah.

Khomeini and His Influence

Playing on the Twelver Shiites' expectation of the return of the Twelfth Imam, Khomeini claimed to be a linear descendant of Ali and took for himself the title of Imam. He was thus able to stir up the emotions of the people and broaden his power base. Ayatollah Khomeini was successful in deposing the shah and recreating Iran so that it would conform to his ideology. He built a state in which the clergy has absolute control; there is no secular authority with which to contend.

Not content with changing Iran, Khomeini attempted to export his concept of religious government. His propaganda calling for the downfall of Saddam Hussein in Iraq resulted in an eight-year border war. However, the Shiite majority in Iraq did not seem prepared for Khomeini's style of government and did not withdraw support from Hussein, though perhaps out of fear.

Both countries paid a heavy toll for the conflict, financially and in the lives of citizens. The Iranian and Iraqi economies fell into shambles as a result of financing that long war. Iran had sent every able-bodied male into battle. At the Ramadi prisoner of war (POW) camp about sixty-five miles west of Baghdad, Iraq, prisoners ranged in age from thirteen-year-old boys to white-haired old men. One of the youngest prisoners tearfully described how he had been given three months of training before being sent to the front near Khorramshahr. He and his Iranian fellows had been told the Iraqis were all heathens and that it was their holy duty to fight them.

To stir up the Shiites in Iraq, Khomeini declared that Saddam Hussein was Muawiya (the original antagonist of Ali fourteen hundred years ago) coming back from the grave to kill Khomeini. What Khomeini subtly communicated was that he was Ali—the Prophet's true successor.

Though Khomeini is dead, there is a well-organized network throughout the Arab world of Khomeini-type radicals who promote Khomeini's ideas by selling his Arabic tapes in almost every capital city in the Middle East.

Engineer Muhammad Abdel Salam Farag, author of the book *The Missing Religious Duty* and one of the five accused assassins of Anwar Sadat, was influenced greatly by Khomeini's ideas.

The Danger for the Future

As Iran continues to export its brand of Islamic government, the possibility exists that the more-moderate Sunni governments around the Persian Gulf will be overthrown by radical Shiites (or, at the very least, that Sunni governments will become more radical in an effort to appease their Shiite populations). As noted earlier, a coup has already been attempted in Bahrain, and Iraq's invasion of Kuwait has sent shivers down the spine of the Saudis in their rich kingdom.

We have seen how Islamic fundamentalist ideology, regardless of the different branches of Islam, is anti-Western and anti-Christian. The ideology as a whole is dedicated to dominating the allegiance of all mankind.

But it is also true that some Muslims are more ideologically oriented than others—that some, like Shiites responsive to the teachings of Khomeini, are more passionately opposed than others to the West and everything about it. Others, who are materially motivated, like Saddam Hussein, can use Islam as a cover for personal ideology. If such people take control of more of the oil-rich nations in the Middle East, the status of our vital oil supplies from those states would be far less secure. It is almost certain that the wealth of those nations would be used to promote Islamic superiority even more aggressively than at present.

The questions are being echoed from coast to coast here in the United States: "Is oil worth the spilling of American blood? Can we not bite the bullet and develop our oil reserves through off-shore drilling shells instead? By using off-shore drilling, it may cost $60 a barrel for the first consuming generation, but wouldn't we have enough oil at that price to meet America's need for the next 500 years?"

These questions will no doubt be debated hotly for years to come.

CHAPTER 6

EGYPT: CASE OF A CONQUERED NATION

Many scholars have argued that Egypt can be seen as an illustration of what happens to a nation when fundamentalist Islam becomes so influential. Similar stories could be told about other Muslim states. Typically, only Muslims are regarded as full citizens with all the rights of citizenship.

*E*gypt is a poignant case study of the way Islam can drown a nation. It serves as an example of what happens when Islamic revolutionaries call for revival. The power struggle between radical Muslims and the moderate leadership of any modern Muslim state is inevitable; the two forces cannot peacefully coexist. Egypt's moderate leaders have tried continually to align themselves with the West—not only to loosen the Russian hold on their land and economy but also to hold off militant revolutionaries who threaten political stability. The West, for its part, saw Egypt as a replacement of the Shah of Iran and poured its hopes for the Middle East into Egypt, counting on its pro-Western leadership to give impetus and direction for a comprehensive peace settlement.

Since President Anwar Sadat's assassination, however, disconcerting questions have arisen: How well-founded is that hope for peace now? Was a man or an idea killed? Was Sadat's assassination an isolated incident without implications? Or was it part of the same pattern of anti-modernistic, anti-Western Islamic resurgence that swept Iran and Libya, Iraq and Syria.

President Hosni Mubarak, Sadat's hand-picked successor, vowed "no change" in government policies established by Sadat. But can he continue to steer a moderate course through the middle of the mounting tensions and conflicts in Egyptian society? Sadat was hated both inside and outside his country by Islamic fundamentalists, who are increasing in numbers as well as in fervor.

Peace Mission and Death Warrant

When Anwar Sadat traveled to Jerusalem in November 1977 on his mission for peace in the Middle East, he stirred the fury of the Islamic world against him. In the eyes of the West, Sadat's peace initiative was an act of vision, courage, and statesmanship of the highest order. To great numbers of Muslims, however, Sadat had committed high treason. They interpreted the independent gesture by which he sought an end to the continual hatred, war, and violence of the Arab-Israeli blood-feud as a betrayal. Not only did he break the twenty-nine-year-old Arab ban on direct dealings with the Israelis, which had existed since the founding of the State of Israel in 1948, but his declared willingness, proclaimed to Israel's Knesset, "to live with you in permanent peace and justice," amounted to heresy in the minds of many of his fellow Muslims.

Until Sadat's pilgrimage, no leader on either side had taken such a radical step forward on the road to peace. His bold trip to Jerusalem and the negotiations that followed became the means for breaking the political deadlock of the preceding three decades.

The peace process he inaugurated bore its first fruit at Camp David, Maryland, where Sadat, Israeli Prime Minister Menachem Begin, and United States President Jimmy Carter sequestered themselves for thirteen days in September 1978 and hammered out the historic "framework for peace." More lengthy and precarious negotiations followed while the rest of the world watched and waited. Finally, on March 26, 1979, at an emotional White House ceremony, the three leaders signed a formal treaty. For the first time in thirty-one years, Egypt and Israel were no longer in a state of war.

However, it was a costly irony. When Sadat signed the peace treaty, he also, in effect, signed his own death warrant. The Islamic world wanted him dead. Peace-loving people of all nationalities were stunned and grief-stricken when President Sadat was assassinated on October 6, 1981, by a band of Muslim fanatics. But while some mourned his loss and paid him tribute, great throngs in many Islamic countries took to the streets, rejoicing in the "death of the infidel."

"Sadat was doomed from the day he went to Jerusalem," declared Lieutenant General Saadeddin Shazli, one of Egypt's most famous political exiles. "Anyone who follows in the traitorous path will similarly be doomed."

His assassins were extremists, but their action was not really surprising. It was a deliberate attempt to purify Islam, to eliminate what they considered a corrupt element.

What We Need to Understand

A strain of Western thinkers, who are more idealistic than pragmatic, want to accommodate the Islamic mixing of religion and politics. Yet they would surely be the ones screaming all the way to the Supreme Court if Christians in the U.S. tried to do the same thing. Those same thinkers are the ones who ask simplistic questions such as the following: What is wrong with an attempt to square political conduct with religious principles? Isn't it understandable, even laudable, for leaders to try to remodel public and private life?

This attitude assumes there is no reason why the West's encounters with militant Islam ultimately should be unpleasant. After all, Islam is monotheistic and one of the world's higher religions.

Such reasoning ignores the philosophy of Islamic literalism that makes militant Islam both powerful and dangerous, as illustrated throughout this book.

Islamic purists divide the world into two camps—believers and infidels. Infidels are to be humiliated, denied due process of law, and ultimately, converted or killed. Islam's simple vindication of this is found in the Koran:

> Fight against such of those who have been given the Scripture as believe not in Allah nor the Last day. . . . (9:29)

No genuine Christian reformer could pursue such a philosophy and remain true to Christian doctrine. But to follow such a strategy is precisely what makes a Muslim true to Islam. Using this same scripture as justification, Muslim zealots consider moderate Muslims, who do not follow the letter of the law, to be infidels also, equally deserving the same treatment.

By its philosophy and style, the Muslim Brotherhood of Egypt is an example of the type of radical movements that exist in virtually every Islamic state. (Such radical movements, of course, exist in virtually every world religion.) Radical Islamic groups are religious organizations bent on applying Islamic law literally. Founder of the Egyptian Muslim Brotherhood, Hasan Al-Banna, forcefully expressed the viewpoint of those groups to his followers:

> You are not a benevolent organization, nor a political party, nor a local association with limited aims. Rather, you are a new spirit making its way into the heart of this nation, and reviving it through the Koran; a new light dawning and scattering the darkness of materialism through the knowledge of God; a resounding

voice rising and echoing the message of the Apostle.[1]

The extreme sense of religious superiority these groups exhibit has created problems with Islam itself. Shukri Ahmed Mustafa, a leader of the Muslim Brotherhood offshoot group accused in the killing of the former Egyptian minister of Trusts and Bequests, said his movement's philosophy was based on "sacred hatred" of Islamic nations he believes have departed from the true faith. "Spilling the blood of heretics is the sacred duty of all Muslims," Mustafa told a reporter before he was hanged in 1978. Indeed, the assassination of President Sadat was a part of an old pattern of attempts to prod the masses into Islamic revolution that would lead to the "Islamic Republic of Egypt."

The Muslim Brotherhood of Egypt did not come to the world's attention until Sadat was killed, but it existed long before the tragic event catapulted it to notoriety. While the Brotherhood is far from a majority movement in Egypt, it exerts much influence. Founded in 1928, it is dedicated to establishing a modern political community based on a return to the fundamental precepts of Islam. In the fifties, the Brotherhood rapidly gained such power that President Gamal Abdel Nasser imprisoned its leaders and many members of the group were placed in

---

1 Hasan Al-Banna, "Between Yesterday and Today," *Five Tracts of Hasan Al-Banna*, Trans. Charles Wendell (Berkeley: University of California Press), 36.

concentration camps or hanged because of assassination attempts on Nasser. Imprisonment and hard labor continued for the Brotherhood until President Sadat came to power in 1970. Ironically, Sadat released the Muslim Brotherhood's leaders from prison in an effort to impress the democratic West.

To Islamic purists, such as Brotherhood members, all other religions are either heretical or hopelessly corrupt. They tolerate no other view; they also believe that it is Allah's will for all societies to come under the Islamic flag and for Islamic law and religion to control and undergird all of life for all people. In other words, only a doctrinally pure, incorrupt Islamic nation can please Allah. Anything else must be redeemed or destroyed.

Islam Invades Egypt

Islam first came to Egypt as it did to many traditional Christian lands such as Syria, Palestine, and North Africa: by the Islamic/Arab invasion in the middle 600s A.D.

Today, Egypt's original Christian heritage can be seen only dimly in the lives of an existing minority of Coptics (Egyptians) who refused total submission to the Arab/Islamic conquerors. The high cost of refusal was often their own lives. Few people were able to pay the high taxes the Muslims imposed, so their only alternative (if they wanted to live) was to accept Islam, to become "part of the faithful." Those too poor to pay taxes, yet unwilling to convert to Islam, were martyred.

The largest group to withstand the onslaught of Islam was the Coptic church in Egypt. Founded in A.D. 42 by Mark, the author of the second Gospel, the Coptic church had six hundred years to become established before the Muslims overran Egypt. The Copts have retained much of their original heritage, and with seven million members, they make up 10 to 15 percent of the Egyptian population.

Life has not ceased to be difficult for the Copts in modern times. Radical Islamic organizations are trying to pressure the government to return to the concept of the *dhimmi*, thereby making Copts second-class citizens.

The Muslim Brotherhood and other radical Muslim groups have made Egyptian Copts a special target for their violence. Property is destroyed; people are beaten, maimed, and killed. For example, since August 14, 1977, Muslims have destroyed Christian shops, restaurants, homes, a cathedral, as well as Protestant churches.

Most of this violence is an expression of frustration against the pro-Western government by Islamic fundamentalists. Why is it aimed at Christians? They are not only an easy target, but to the fundamentalists, Christianity in Egypt is an expression of Western and infidel values.

Egyptian Law

Often the government, in trying to walk a tightrope, ends up offending both groups. For example, in the town of Basatten, near Cairo, a church was seized by a radical Muslim organization. The Muslims converted it into a mosque. When the Christians complained to the authorities that their property had been taken, the police demolished the building because the Christians had not had the proper construction permits.

Egyptian law states that no church may be built or have any alterations, repairs, or improvements without a presidential decree. That law was enacted in 1856, following the outline of the "Covenant of Umar." (The statute was placed on the books by the Ottoman Empire when Egypt was one of its colonies.) In 1972, President Anwar Sadat promised Coptic leaders that he would give fifty permits per year for church building. During the period between 1973 and 1979, he gave a total of fifty permits. In 1978 and in 1979, he gave five permits.

By 1990, there were hundreds of outstanding applications for permits that had been accumulating for years. Christian churches have sometimes waited as long as twenty-seven years for a permit to build, while the government builds mosques almost daily and pays mosque leaders. Since taking office, President Mubarak has reactivated and tightened this law, making it impossible for new churches to be erected or old churches to be renovated.

Since 1973, to appease the fundamentalists, Egypt has made progress toward Islamization. Urged on by radical Islamic organizations, legislation is paving the way to make the Koran the major source of law. Court decisions are setting precedents wherein non-Muslims are being pushed more and more into the role of the *dhimmi.*

In response to the government's refusal to adequately respond to Coptic complaints, Pope Shenouda of the Coptic church canceled all official Easter festivities for 1980. He restricted Easter celebrations to simple prayers. Refusing to accept President Sadat's annual Easter greetings, the pope patriarch and the members of the Holy Synod (the governing body of the church) retired to the desert monastery of St. Bishoy. Angered by the worldwide press attention caused by this and other moves, President Sadat attacked Coptic leaders in a speech on May 14 of that year. He accused them of plotting to overthrow his government, of slandering both him and Egypt, and of attempting to foster social discontent. Sadat then placed the Christian leaders under house arrest at synod from their positions of authority within the church. In their stead, he appointed a council of bishops, which was to be more responsive to governmental policies.

Following the assassination of Sadat in 1981, virtually all of his political prisoners were released, including leaders of the Muslim Brotherhood. President Mubarak a few years later released the Coptic leaders and allowed them to resume their duties as the ruling body of the church.

Only One Example

Many scholars have argued that Egypt can be seen as an illustration of what happens to a nation when fundamentalist Islam becomes so influential. Similar stories could be told about other Muslim states. Typically, only Muslims are regarded as full citizens with all the rights of citizenship. In Saudi Arabia, for example, non-Muslims cannot be citizens at all. Also in Saudi Arabia, no Christian churches of any kind can be built.

Those policies followed by Islamic fundamentalism are consistent with the Muslim mandate to convert. To the Muslim there is only one true religion (Islam), so there are no such things as freedom of religion or separation of church and state. Religious restrictions are the natural outgrowth of a faith which demands that all the world be brought under its banner. Just as those policies and practices have been implemented in many Islamic countries, they will be put into effect in any other nation that comes under Muslim domination.

CHAPTER 7

ISRAEL, ISLAM, AND THE WEST[1]

Today's Modern Islamic zealots and their Muslim brethren before them have repeatedly sworn that there can be no peace with Israel. "It is," they say, "a constant reminder of the Westerner's humiliation to Muslims."

1 This chapter was first written as chapter 6, "The State of Israel and The Deepening of the Tension Between Islam and The West," in my book, *Revolt Against Modernity* (Leiden: E. J. Brill, 1985) and is used here, with minor revisions, with permission from E. J. Brill.

Western support of the creation of the State of Israel on the soil of Islamic Arab Palestine became further incrimination of the West's perceived hostility toward Islam.

The American occupation and support of the State of Israel from its inception in 1948 has raised many "Aha's" among Muslims from Morocco to Jakarta. Those Muslims who believed the West hated them saw this as one more means of Western humiliation.

How Did It All Happen?

During World War I, the Balfour Declaration was the price Britain paid to gain worldwide Jewish backing for the war effort. At that time Great Britain urgently needed every possible source of support. Russia had dropped out of the war because of the 1917 revolution. Since many leaders of the new anti-war leftist Soviet government were Jewish, it was feared that their co-religionists would support the revolutionary cause rather than the Czarist regime backed by the Allies. Some British leaders even hoped to win German-Jewish support away from the Kaiser.

Late in 1936, wartime Prime Minister David Lloyd George revealed that the Zionists had promised to rally Jewish pro-Allied sentiment if they received a commitment to establish a Jewish national home in Palestine. "They were helpful," he commented in the House of Commons.[2] The declaration took the form of a public letter from Lord Balfour, the British Foreign Minister, to Lord Rothschild, a prominent English leader in Jewish causes. It stated:

> "His Majesty's government views with favor the establishment in Palestine of a national home for the Jewish people and would use their best endeavors to facilitate the achievement of this object. It being clearly understood that nothing shall be done which may prejudice the civil and religious rights of existing non-Jewish communities in Palestine, or the rights and political status enjoyed by Jews in any other country."[3]

---

2 Don Peretz, *The Middle East Today* (New York: Holt, Rinehart, and Winston, 1978), 101.
3 Peretz, *The Middle East Today.*

Palestine

Palestine was an anomaly. Its Jewish and Arab populations were among the most politically sophisticated and culturally developed in the area. Conflict between Jewish and Arab nationalism, however, frustrated all British attempts to encourage local self-government. Arab nationalists considered Palestine part of the Arab heartland and refused to surrender any of their rights or claims. Zionists, on the other hand, envisioned Palestine as a Jewish national home and were determined to realize that aspiration. The devious dealings and duplicity of the British operation did not help the situation. The promise of the officer at the foreign office in Cairo would be diametrically opposed to that of the foreign secretary in London; this kept the Arabs and the Zionists guessing all the time.

To illustrate, the British tried to stop the Zionists from expansion when the Arab nationalists pressured them; similarly, when the Jewish lobby in Britain counter-pressured the British, they, in turn, leaned on the Arabs.

Britain came to feel what they called the "dual obligation." On one hand, they tried to accommodate the pressure of Zionists whose power in England showed at the ballot box and, on the other hand, they tried to appease the Arabs, whose satisfaction the British felt obligated to ensure.

The details of the British dealings under this "dual obligation" understandably cemented Islamic/Arab suspicion toward the Christian West.

Zionism: The European Beginning

Modern Zionism, inspired by the ancient land of Israel of the Old Testament, is the movement that calls for a Jewish return to the homeland. Zionism was a direct product of the economic, political, and social conditions of nineteenth-century European Jews. Indirectly, Zionism was the culmination of the many centuries of Jewish history that followed the dispersion of the Palestinian Jewish community after the Roman conquest of the first century A.D. From the Holy Land, Jews emigrated or were transported to Europe, for the most part, where they usually lived together in communities separate from the Europeans and practiced the laws, traditions, and customs of ancient Israel.

Despite generations of living in other countries, they remained, in essence, foreigners. It is no surprise, therefore, that when the idea of a homeland became a reality, thousands of them flocked to Israel from most European countries. The Jews, then, were isolated from the community at large and frequently expelled en masse. Nearly every major European nation—Spain, France, England, Poland, Romania, and Germany—exiled its Jewish community at one time or another.

"The Jews," Herzl wrote, "would always be persecuted no matter how useful or patriotic they were. Nowhere was their integration into national life possible; the Jewish problem, the hatred of the Jewish minority by non-Jewish majority, existed wherever there were

Jews. Even immigration to hopefully safe places did not exempt Jews from eventual anti-Semitism."[4]

In 1914, there were some six hundred thousand Arabs and eighty-five thousand Jews in Palestine. The Arabs had not as yet developed any nationalistic feeling because it was their loyalty to Islam or Christianity, not the state, which dominated. A distinctive Arab and later Palestinian common nationalist movement did not emerge until World War I. Osmanlis (Turkey) exercised only a shadow of control over many parts of Palestine. The Bedouin still roamed and periodically raided the settled villages in the hill country on the northern plains.

Immediately after the outbreak of World War I, the Osmanlis (the Ottomans) clamped rigid restrictions on Palestine and the surrounding area. In addition to the harsh treatment, widespread drought and a locust plague caused a famine. Foreign minorities fared worse than others at the hand of the Ottoman government because they had lost the protection accorded minorities from payments to the government, payments that had been abolished by the Osmanlis in 1914.

The unrest of Arab nationalists within and beyond the borders of Palestine forced the British to clarify their position in Winston Churchill's white paper of July 1922. It maintained that Arab fears were caused by "exaggerated interpretations" of the Balfour Declaration and "unauthorized statements" that Palestine would become wholly Jewish. Churchill's statement drew atten-

4 Ibid, 259.

tion to the fact that the Balfour Declaration did not acknowledge "that Palestine as a whole should be converted into a Jewish national home, but that such a home should be found in Palestine." All citizens of the country were Palestinian, and none were entitled to any special judicial status.

On the other hand, to allay Jewish apprehensions, Churchill affirmed that the Balfour promises would not be abandoned. He explained that the Balfour Declaration did not entail an imposition of Jewish nationality on all the country's inhabitants, but simply the continued political and economic development of the existing Jewish community with the help of world Jewry.

Great Britain's de jure position in Palestine was confirmed by the Lausanne Peace Treaty with Turkey in 1923, although the League of Nations had already assigned the Palestinian mandate in July 1922. It differed from the other Middle East mandates that called for progressive development of independent states. In Palestine, the British were vested with "full powers of legislation and of administration save as they may be limited by the terms of this mandate."[5] The mandate did not mention the Arab community.

The mandate also authorized Jewish immigration and "closed settlement" on the land. Jews who decided to establish permanent residence would be assisted in obtaining Palestinian citizenship. Jewish community

---

5 P. M. Holt, *Egypt and The Fertile Crescent 1516–1922* (Ithaca and London: Cornell University Press, 1966), 292.

leaders were authorized to construct and operate public works, services, and utilities not directly undertaken by mandatory administration.

Both Jewish and Arab communities complained that the British mandatory authorities discriminated against them. Both protested any measure intended to lead toward self-government: the Arabs because the measures were not drastic enough; the Jews because the measures appeared to favor the Arabs.

Torn between Arab and Jewish demands, the mandatory officials attempted to balance one side against the other, further evidence to add to the Muslim's distrust. Some British thought the implementation of the mandate would jeopardize Great Britain's friendship with other Muslim nations by antagonizing the Arabs and thus would be impossible. Others regarded the Jewish community as a progressive element that could serve as an example of modernization to the whole Middle East. Thus, policy fluctuated on all levels according to whims and prejudices of local officials.

In this kind of environment, the antagonists became increasingly bitter toward one another and toward the mandatory power, until the gaps became unbridgeable. Each community went its own way, developing its separate institutions in violent conflict with those of the other.

Despite the formal existence of Palestinian citizenship, Palestinian government, and Palestinian officialdom, there was really no Palestinian community. Instead, on one side the British official life operated in its own framework of military and administrative organization, while on the other side the Arab community, with its growing national movement, fused the Muslim and various Christian communities under the control of the leading Muslim families. The Arab self-governing institutions often supplemented the functions of British mandatory government.

The British role in creating the state of Israel and, later, America's recognition of that state have left a deep scar in the body of the Arab Muslim world. That is the reason this particular period of history has received a careful and thorough consideration. Arabs and, in particular, Muslim activists are certain that the Christian West has implanted Israel in their midst to keep control of the area. This thought interwoven with four hundred years of Crusades has convinced them that the Christian West has never respected their dignity.

Muslims, unlike Westerners, cannot forget the past very easily. To them the Crusades happened yesterday. To them colonialism still exists in the form of the state of Israel and, thus, the United States and Western Europe are to be blamed for every conceivable problem in the Middle East. These are not just wild accusations; they are deeply felt convictions. Most Muslim activists are mindful of the duplicity of the British and the French agreement to divide the Arab nations between them like a loaf of bread. England got Palestine, Iraq, Egypt, and modern Jordan. France claimed Lebanon, Syria, Algiers, Morocco, and Tunisia.

The thought of "the House of War," namely Israel,

occupying a land that belongs to the House of Islam is no small matter to Muslim revolutionaries. For it smacks at the heart of their religious ideologies.

Today's Modern Islamic zealots and their Muslim brethren before them have repeatedly sworn that there can be no peace with Israel. "It is," they say, "a constant reminder of the Westerner's humiliation to Muslims." They planted their own base in a Muslim land, and Islam cannot rest until the Jews either leave "Palestine" or accept rulership by a Muslim government.

CHAPTER 8

MEETING THE CHALLENGE OF ISLAM

If we are to win Muslims to Jesus Christ, we must show them the true moral strength of Western Christian heritage. We must show them living examples of godliness and caring.

*U*nlike other religions, Islam has as one of its most basic tenets the endless pursuit of *jihad*, the ongoing holy war being fought for conversion and domination, and all true Muslims believe in it and pursue it to some extent or another. Thus, even so-called moderate Muslim leaders have this underlying determination in their dealings with the West. There is a large and growing radical element in Islam that is even more bent on holy war and would use more aggressively the Arabs' great oil supplies and wealth as weapons in that war.

Already the spread of Islam is impressive—and threatening. The Muslims' well-funded evangelistic efforts have been so successful to date that Muslims expect to be dominant in Europe within the next few decades; furthermore, they expect to become the world's largest religion in that same time period. Their growing influence is also evident here in the United

States, where mosques are being erected in major cities, including a replica of the Dome of the Rock mosque (the original is in Jerusalem) going up in suburban Phoenix, Arizona. The history of Egypt and other countries gives us a good example of what can happen to freedom of religion in a country dominated by Islam.

Another potential danger is the high level of Islamic (primarily Arab) investment in the West, with the accompanying threat of economic disruption. As discussed earlier, Muslims do not hesitate to use their wealth to force conversion to Islam, or to force non-Muslims to comply with Islamic laws.

Faced with these facts, how do we react? How do we face the challenge of resurgent Islam and its invasion of the West? What measures would be appropriate and effective?

These are important questions, and no one, no matter how knowledgeable, has all the answers. Yet common sense and thorough historical examinations will prompt us to try to implement some simple, yet demanding, steps to avoid making the same mistake others have made.

First, Westerners must seek to understand the character and objectives of modern Islamic fundamentalism and the serious threat it poses to their way of life. The ignorance and naivete of most Westerners regarding Islam is alarming. Thus, the first thing the West must do is to become informed. People who are aware of the problem, especially Christians, must speak up in warning. Our governments, churches, and mass media need to be alerted to the truth of the situation. All individuals and groups who know what is happening share the responsibility for informing the Western public.

Second, the United States must tear itself loose from dependence on OPEC oil. While the United States is the world's largest oil importer, the Soviet Union is the world's largest oil producer and is virtually energy self-sufficient.

Some continue to think America should not strive for energy independence. The cost would be too high, they say, and it would result in social disruption since it would reduce energy consumption substantially. Their approach to the problem is for Americans to do what they do best and let the Arabs do what they do best. The United States is more efficient at producing wheat and computers, they reason, and thus it would retain a bargaining leverage with OPEC.

That view, however, is too simplistic. It assumes a world in which everything is measured in dollars and mathematical formulas. If that were reality, such a plan would make sense. But again, it illustrates Western naivete about the religious dimension. Muslim states are made up of people who believe that to die in opposing the infidel is to earn oneself instant paradise.

America is not moving faster toward energy self-sufficiency because it does not take seriously the need to do so. The government's efforts to build a better energy base are being negated by special interests. As long as the point of focus of our energy policy is short term, our nation will not come close to energy independence. And, unfortunately, those looking at the short term will continue to see a relatively simple world where Muslims, Christians, and Jews share religious roots and, therefore, to a greater or lesser degree, will be able to live harmoniously with one another. But as long as "the House of Islam versus the House of War" mentality exists, there can be no peace between Muslims and their enemies.

Third, countries such as the United States must tighten foreign investment laws. The fear that Arab investors could bring down the American economy by yanking out their funds was the theme of the film *Rollover.* Imagine the chaos in American commercial centers if OPEC investors suddenly liquidated their assets, dumped their United States Treasury bills on the market, or transferred their liquid assets away from the United States. It is conceivable that extreme damage could be done to many sectors of the American economy by wild, dramatic financial manipulations by foreign investors.

Exactly how our investment laws should be modified is a matter for experts. But every nation has the right to protect its economy from manipulation by foreign investors, and safeguards are clearly needed.

On the other hand, everyone doing business with Muslim governments or individuals needs to make sure there are no religious strings attached to such dealings. Even then there are no foolproof ways to determine, for example, how a farmland or a bank is going to be used after it is sold. Westerners must never forget that more than economics is involved when doing business with a Muslim.

Therefore, we need to be as "wise as serpents" in the use of our resources. Islam spread through North Africa, Syria, Egypt, and Iran by the implementation of the concept of *jihad*. But into Africa and far into Asia, Islam spread by a different method: commerce and trading. Thus, when the editorial page of *Al Ahram* newspaper (the official newspaper of Egypt) called for Arabs to use their muscle of $200 billion in the United States to get what they wanted, it became history repeating itself, rather than a mere prejudiced, alarmist misconception.

Fourth, the United States government must urge all countries to allow all of their citizens full human rights. It is illegal to be a citizen of certain Islamic countries, such as Saudi Arabia, unless one is a Muslim. Further, Christians, Jews, and members of other faiths are often (and in some nations always) forbidden to build churches.

The nations of the Christian West (the United States in particular) have declared themselves to be the protectors of the oppressed. How about using whatever influence we have to help Christians, Jews, and other minorities in all countries of the Middle East, including Israel?

Fifth, while in the West religious freedom is afforded all groups, including Muslims, Western governments must not allow anti-democratic Islamic laws to be incorporated into their bodies of law, which are based largely on Judeo-Christian values. In other words, Islamic freedom and growth in the West must not be allowed to be like "the camels in the tent," ultimately taking away the freedom of most.

Finally, Christians must accept the challenge of Islam as a specifically religious challenge—in short, Christians need to practice what they preach. Western Christians boast that their societies are built on the foundation of Judeo-Christian ethics. If that is so, we should live both individually and collectively as Christians. We must learn the principle of loving those with whom we disagree theologically. On an international level, we must seek to love those who hate and condemn us. I am not suggesting that we become weak or passive. Firmness and compassion are not mutually exclusive. We must speak and act with authority, yet without arrogance.

In a world of confusion, especially in the Middle East where growing pains are coupled with overt enmity between Muslims and Jews, the West should have clear and crisp objectives, firm and coherent policies. We should be straightforward and honest even when we disagree. We should construct our foreign policy on a firm basis of justice rather than on the basis of economic or political interests. If we don't begin to act this way, the Muslim world rightly can continue to perceive the West as typically materialistic. This only increases the danger of the flow of oil being disrupted.

The West must brace itself and plan ahead for still more resurgence of Islamic extremism. What we saw in Iran and now in Iraq is merely the tip of the iceberg. As Muslim nations develop greater monetary power, adjustments and disturbances in society will become more evident and will overflow into political and religious life. As the Muslim nations, in general, and the Arab nations, in particular, try to express their independence in various ways, the West must convince them that we are friends, not foes.

The United States and Europe have given hundreds of millions of dollars in aid to several Muslim nations, but this fact often goes unnoticed by the general populace. The West should increase its public relations efforts to show the good things Western nations are doing for the world, specifically the Muslim world.

Muslims have continued to reject the Western lifestyle. We are partially to blame for that. Too often Americans and other Westerners—seen as the Christians in the world—display the shallow and superficial aspects of our culture. Muslims see how we live, regardless of what we say. Because of our actions, Muslims are frankly not interested in the Christian faith.

If we are to win Muslims to Jesus Christ, we must show them the true moral strength of Western Christian heritage. We must show them living examples of godliness and caring.